A NOTE:

It was amazing — and gratifying — to see how people reacted to the first TV Theme Song book. Obviously I'm not the only one who remembers these "modern folk songs" fondly; in fact, this volume exists today because people insisted on more. Specifically, the most frequently requested additional themes were (can you guess?): *Rawhide, Gilligan's Island, Patty Duke,* and *Sugarfoot* (which surprised me). But everyone seems to have a special favorite. I hope yours is included. If not, well . . . there's always next time! Have fun and **sing out loud!** JJ.

ACKNOWLEDGMENTS

- I've been very lucky to have had Bob Miller as my editor, friend, and supporter for the last five years. He and I both know that this book would never have been written if he hadn't insisted. For that, and for all of his help with all of my books, I'm grateful. Thanks, Bob — let's make it at least another five.
- The folks at Hal Leonard Publishing, particularly Mary Bultman (whose patience is astounding) and Glenda Herro, get a big kiss. Except Keith and Dave, who get *Rawhide* hand-shakes.
- Lloyd Jassin, my publicist at St. Martin's, has been a blessing and a good friend. Next time I go to Pittsburgh, I'm taking you with me, Lloyd. Keep up the great work!
- Thanks to Eric Lefcowitz for hanging in there.
- You're in here too, Sharon. Love American Style.
- 2nd Annual Citation for performance above and beyond the call of duty: Mary Kay Landon, Vicki Rombs, Lisa DiMona.
- Thank you Dan Acree for the fantastic publicity job.
- *Father Knows Best* is for Tom Shales. I didn't know there were lyrics either.
- *Davy Crockett* is for Douglas Durden, wherever she is.
- *Love Boat* is especially for Dick Bright, who epitomizes everything that's fun about TV Themes.
- Bill Frank at ASCAP and Charles Pavlosky at BMI came through again. You guys are terrific!
- My agents, Joyce (the Phantom) Cole and Jayne (First National) Walker, get a big hug.
- Thanks to Lonnie Graham for the pop culture psychology.
- Thanks to my two TV Theme experts: Steve Gelfand and Roger Dorfman. I was lucky to find you both.
- Rollin, rollin, rollin, thanks to Ron and Roland (as always).
- Special thanks to Arlene Muller for her kindness and assistance.
- Thank you Bob Denver and Jose Feliciano, and all the people who made the theme songs available to me: Rick Hansen. Michael Goldsen, John Gart, David Newell, J. R. Rogers, Joan Schulman, Paul Barry, Sidney Herman, Bob Wright,
- *Gidget* is for Jim Kerr. Now we can *both* sing it!
- Thanks to Andy Carpenter for his time and energy in helping me make choices. I appreciate it!
- Thanks to Josh Marwell for his enthusiasm and support.
- Harry Trumbore can be Top Cat this time.

Table Of Contents

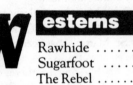

THE TV THEME SONG
SING~ALONG SONG BOOK
Volume 2

By John Javna

Designed by
Ron Addad & Roland Addad

Published by
Hal Leonard Publishing Corporation / St. Martin's Press
175 Fifth Avenue
New York, NY 10010

THIS BOOK IS WARMLY DEDICATED TO THE SALES FORCE OF
ST. MARTIN'S PRESS, WHO MADE TV THEMES, VOLUME 1,
A SUCCESS STORY

OTHER BOOKS BY JOHN JAVNA:

- *60s!* (with Gordon Javna)
- *How To Jitterbug*
- *The TV Theme Song Sing-Along Song Book*
- *Cult TV*

THIS BOOK WAS CREATED AND PACKAGED BY J-BIRD PRESS

TYPESETTING BY: KAZAN Typeset Services
PASTE-UP BY: Vicki Rombs

John Javna, professor of TV Theme-ology

THE TV THEME SONG SING-ALONG SONGBOOK, VOLUME 2
Copyright © 1985 by John Javna. All rights reserved. Printed in the United States of America. No part of this book may be used or reproduced in any manner whatsoever without written permission except in the case of brief quotations embodied in critical articles or reviews. For information, address St. Martin's Press, 175 Fifth Avenue, New York, NY 10010.

DESIGN BY: Ron Addad and Roland Addad (thanks, guys).
ISBN: 0-312-78218-7
Library of Congress Catalogue Number: 84-758771

First Edition
10 9 8 7 6 5 4 3 2 1

(Revised for volume 2)
Main entry under title:

The TV theme song sing-along songbook.

  1. Television music — United States.   I. Javna, John.
M1527.7.T9 1984   84-758771
ISBN 0-312-78215-2 (pbk. : v. 1)
ISBN 0-312-78218-7 (pbk. : v. 2)

Table Of Contents

The Patty Duke Show

THE SHOW: How's this for a genetic miracle: Patty and Cathy Lane just *happen* to be identical cousins. But that's about all they have in common. Cathy, who's from Scotland, is living with her uncle's family in Brooklyn Heights, New York, while her parents are abroad. She's a shy, refined 16-year-old trying to adjust to the American way of life. Patty, on the other hand, is a typical American teenager who's in love with slumber parties, hot dogs, and rock' n'roll. Naturally everyone gets the look-alike cousins confused, even Patty's parents: Martin, a newspaper editor with the *New York Chronicle*, and Natalie. But the girls manage to use this to their advantage. Every time one of them gets into trouble (usually Patty), they switch identities and bluff their way out of it.

Patty Duke was 17 years old when she first appeared as as Patty and Cathy Lane

THE SONG: One of the best-remembered theme songs of the '60s. Favorite line: "a hot dog makes her lose control…"

Main Cast

Patty Lane: Patty Duke
Cathy Lane (her cousin): Patty Duke
Martin Lane (her father): William Schallert
Natalie Lane (her mother): Jean Byron
Ross Lane (her brother): Paul O'Keefe
Richard Harrison (her boyfriend): Eddie Applegate
Ted Brownley (Cathy's boyfriend): Skip Hinnant
J. R. Castle (Martin's boss): John McGiver
Sue Ellen (Patty's rival): Kitty Sullivan

Vital Statistics

Half-hour sitcom. ABC. 104 episodes.
First aired: Sept. 18, 1963
Most popular time slot: Wednesday, 8:00-8:30 PM
Last show: Aug. 31, 1966
Ranked in a year's Top 25: 1964 (18)

INSIDE FACTS

PATTY DUKE'S AMAZING CAREER:

- At age 12, she starred as Helen Keller in the Broadway play, *The Miracle Worker*. She gave 994 live performances.
- Her 995th performance was in the film adaptation of the play.
- It won her an Oscar as Best Supporting Actress in 1962.
- In 1979 she won another award for the play: an Emmy (for the TV version). This time she switched roles — to Helen's teacher, Anne Sullivan.
- At 17, she was the youngest performer in television history to have a prime-time series named for her (1963).

TRIVIA QUIZ

THE SUBJECT IS … DOUBLES

Patty Duke played her own cousin. Other TV actors and actresses have played their own relatives in regular series, too. Can you name the shows?
1. James Garner played the hero and his "Pappy" on …
2. Carolyn Jones doubled as her sister Ophelia on …
3. Max Baer, Jr. went in drag to play his character's sister on …
4. Barbara Eden played the title character and her sister on …
5. Elizabeth Montgomery caused trouble for herself as her cousin Serena on …

ANSWERS
1. *Maverick*
2. *The Addams Family*
3. *The Beverly Hillbillies*
4. *I Dream of Jeannie*
5. *Bewitched*

6

The Patty Duke Theme ("Cousins")

Words: Bob Welles, Music: Sig Ramin

Meet Cathy who's lived most everywhere,
From Zanzibar to Berk'ly Square,
But Patty's only seen the sights
A girl can see from Brooklyn Heights,
What a crazy pair!

Where Cathy adores a minuet,
The Ballet Russe and crepe suzette,
Our Patty loves her rock'n'roll,
A hot dog makes her lose control.
What a wild duet!

7

But they're cousins,
Identical cousins all the way,
One pair of matching book-ends,
Diff'rent as night and day.

Still they're cousins,
Identical cousins and you'll find
They laugh alike, they walk alike,
At times they even talk alike,
You can lose your mind,
When cousins are two of a kind.

The Mary Tyler Moore Show

Almost everyone in the Mary Tyler Moore Show went on to star in their own TV series. Two of the alumni: Ed Asner (Lou Grant), and Valerie Harper (Rhoda)

THE SHOW: In the seventies, when America's ideas about women were changing, Mary Richards was the perfect TV role model. Unlike other sitcom females, she wasn't married (or divorced). She didn't have kids. She wasn't young, glamorous, or goofy. Instead, she was capable and independent . . . and at work, she was the boss (except for Lou, of course). Mary had moved to Minneapolis to become an associate news producer at WJM-TV, the lowest-rated station in the Twin Cities. But even *she* couldn't help make them more successful: WJM was stuck with inept Ted Baxter ("Hi guys") as its anchorman. So in the end, she suffered the fate of every TV executive — in the last episode, she was fired along with the rest of the WJM staff . . . except Ted!

THE SONG: Written and sung by Sonny Curtis, an original member of Buddy Holly's Crickets. It was released as a single twice — in 1970, and in 1980, when it was a minor country-western hit.

Main Cast

Mary Richards: Mary Tyler Moore
Lou Grant (her boss): Edward Asner
Ted Baxter (anchorman): Ted Knight
Murray Slaughter (newswriter): Gavin MacLeod
Rhoda Morganstern (Mary's friend): Valerie Harper
Phyllis Lindstrom (Mary's friend): Cloris Leachman
Sue Anne Nevins: Betty White
Georgette Franklin (Ted's girlfriend): Georgia Engel

Vital Statistics

Half-hour sitcom. CBS.
First aired: September 19, 1970
Most popular time slot: Saturday 9:00 – 9:30 PM (1972-76)
Last show: September 3, 1977
Ranked in a year's Top 25: 1971 (22); 1972 (10); 1973 (7); 1974 (9); 1975 (11); 1976 (19)

INSIDE FACTS

MARY'S STRANGE PATH TO STARDOM:
• Her first TV appearance was in a refrigerator ad. She played a 3" tall pixie named Happy Hotpoint, who jumped out of an ice tray saying "Hi, Harriet. Aren't you glad you bought a Hotpoint?"
• Her next big role: a secretary named Sam in *Richard Diamond, Private Detective*. Her face was never seen — only her legs.
• Her *Dick Van Dyke* role came as a fluke: stumped in his search for the right actress to play Laura, producer Sheldon Leonard asked his partner, Danny Thomas: "Don't you know of any *more*?" Thomas remembered *Moore*, who had tried out for the role of the daughter on his sitcom.
• A 1969 TV special prompted CBS to offer her her own show.

TRIVIA QUIZ

A lot of people think they're experts on this show. Are you?
1. Name the address and number of Mary's apartment
2. What channel was WJM-TV?
3. Where did Rhoda work?
4. Where did Ted get his start?
5. How did Chuckles the Clown die?

ANSWERS
5. An elephant shelled him
4. A 5,000 watt radio station in Fresno, CA
3. Hempel's Department Store
2. 12
1. 119 North Weatherly, Apt. D

Love Is All Around

Words and Music: Sonny Curtis

Who can turn the world__ on with her smile,_____

who can take a noth-ing day__ and sud-den-ly make__ it all seem worthwhile?__ Well, it's

you, girl, and you should know__ it, with each glance and ev-'ry lit-tle move-ment you show it.

Love is all a-round, no need to waste __ it. You can have the town; why

don't you take__ it? You're gon-na make it af-ter all._____

9

10

Hogan's Heroes

THE SHOW: Described as "World War II with a laugh track, *Hogan's Heroes* was a funny sitcom in an unfunny setting: a German POW camp. But of course, this was no ordinary prison camp — it was Stalag 13. Headed by bumbling Col. Klink and his portly sidekick Sgt. Schultz ("I know nothing!"), Stalag 13 boasted that no one had ever escaped. The joke was that no one *wanted* to escape! Unknown to Klink, U.S. Air Force Col. Hogan and his band of fellow-prisoners were running a strategic undercover operation right under his nose. Using the name "Papa Bear," the prisoners aided the Allies by securing top-secret information and helping fugitives escape through underground tunnels. Among the heroes: wise-cracking English Cpl. Newkirk and French Cpl. LeBeau, who kept Sgt. Schulz quiet by stuffing him full of fancy French cuisine.

THE SONG: Military march. Lyrics were added later for a record: "Hogan's Heroes Sing the Best of World War II."

Bob Crane played Col. Robert Hogan for almost 6 years, longer than America was actually in World War II!

Main Cast

Col. Robert Hogan: Robert Crane
Col. Wilhelm Klink: Werner Klemperer
Sgt. Hans Schulz: John Banner
Cpl. Louis LeBeau (French): Robert Clary
Cpl. Peter Newkirk (English): Richard Dawson
Lt. Andrew Carter (American): Larry Hovis
Gen. Alfred Burkhalter: Leon Askin

Vital Statistics

Half-hour sitcom. CBS. 168 episodes.
First aired: Sept. 17, 1965
Most popular time slot: Friday, 8:30-9:00 PM (1965-67)
Last show: July 4, 1971
Ranked in a year's Top 25: 1966 (9), 1967 (18)

INSIDE FACTS

ABOUT THE ORIGIN OF HOGAN'S HEROES:

- It was created by Bernard Fein, a former cast-member of *The Phil Silvers Show (Sgt. Bilko)*.
- He originally had it set in an American penitentiary.
- After trying to sell it for four years, he decided to quit show business, and boarded a plane for his hometown, New York City.
- On the plane, he saw someone reading *Von Ryan's Express*, a WW II novel. He flashed on the idea of changing the setting to a P.O.W. camp.
- He immediately flew back to Hollywood, and sold the idea in four days.
- Footnote: the authors of a successful play (and movie) called *Stalag 17* sued the creators of *Hogan's Heroes* for plagiarism and won.

TRIVIA QUIZ

Which star of Hogan's Heroes:
1. Really was a Nazi prisoner during World War II?
2. Fled his native Austria when Hitler invaded it?
3. Played Adolph Eichmann in a film about him?
4. Was mysteriously murdered in 1978?
5. Kissed lots of women on *Family Feud*?

ANSWERS

1. Robert Clary
2. John Banner
3. Werner Klemperer
4. Robert Crane
5. Richard Dawson

The Hogan's Heroes Theme Song

Words and Music by Jerry Fielding

we wish we knew. That's why we he-roes are so few. We've got a

slo-gan from Colo-nel Ho-gan and Colo-nel Ho-gan's a he-ro too,

13

Ne-ver flinch boys, ne-ver be a-fraid he-roes are not born, boys he-roes all are made.

Ask not why boys, ne-ver say die boys, an-swer the call, re-

mem-ber we'll all be he-roes for e-ver-more.

Love, American Style

THE SHOW: What was *Love, American Style* about? Well, it debuted in 1969, so the title wasn't exactly referring to the Cleaver family. But really, folks, it was all pretty innocent. Each program consisted of a bunch of cute one-act plays about love, with titles like "Love and the Practical Joker," "Love and the Legal Agreement," "Love and the Pill" (whoops — guess what *that* one was about . . .). But the real fun for viewers was seeing who the guest stars were each week. You never knew who'd show up — sometimes it was guys your parents would love, like Phyllis Diller and Red Buttons. But other times you could watch Sonny and Cher or Tiny Tim, or sex symbols like Burt Reynolds. Regular features: one-liners and gags by a regular troupe, and "Love-Mate of the Week."

THE SONG: Sung by the Cowsills, it was released as a single — but failed to make the charts.

A typical "love-bird" scene from Love American Style

Vital Statistics

Hour, half-hour. ABC. 65 episodes.
First aired: Sept. 29, 1969
Most popular time slot: Friday, 9:00-10:00 PM (1970, 1971-74)
Last show: Jan. 11, 1974
Never ranked in the Top 25 shows of a year

Main Cast

Regular Repertory Group:
Mary Grover, Richard Williams, Lynne Marta,
Bernie Kopell, Bill Callaway, Phyllis Elizabeth Davis,
Jaki DeMar, Stuart Margolin, Barbara Minkus
Tracy Reed, James Hampton, Buzz Cooper,
Clifton Davis, James A. Watson, Jr., Jed Allen

INSIDE FACTS

"LOVE'S" CHILDREN:
• The pilot of *Happy Days* first appeared as a segment of *Love American Style*.
• It was called "Love and the Happy Day," and featured Ron Howard and Anson Williams as Richie and Potsie.
• *Love American Style* also spawned *The Love Boat*, which copied its format of celebrity skits about love, but tied them together with a uniform setting.
• Bernie Kopell, a member of the regular troupe, later became a regular on *Love Boat* as well.
• Stuart Margolin, another show regular, gained fame (notoriety?) as the unscrupulous "Angel" on *The Rockford Files*.
• 1971 regular Clifton Davis went on to star in his own ABC sitcom 3 years later: *That's My Mama*.

TRIVIA QUIZ

THE SUBJECT IS . . . LOVE

Like *Love, American Style*, these TV series had the word "love" in their titles. Name them.
1. Judy Carne and Peter Deuel starred as young marrieds who lived in a windowless apartment, 1966-71
2. David Birney was Jewish, and Meredith Baxter was Catholic, 1972-73
3. It starred Mr. and Mrs. Arnaz, 1951-57
4. Paul Sand played a bass violin as Robert Dreyfuss, 1974-75
5. Bob Cummings was a bachelor and professional photographer, 1955-59

ANSWERS
5. *Love That Bob*
4. *Friends and Lovers*
3. *I Love Lucy*
2. *Bridget Loves Bernie*
1. *Love On A Rooftop*

Love American Style

Words and Music by Arnold Margolin and Charles Fox

Love American style,
Truer than the red, white and blue.
Love American style,
That's me and you.

And on a star-spangled night, my love
You can rest your head on my shoulder.
While by the dawn's early light, my
    love,
I will defend your right to try.

Love American style,
Freer than the land of the free.
Love American style,
That's you and me.

We pledge our love 'neath the same old
    moon
But it shines red and white and blue
    now.
And in this land of hopes and dreams,
    my love,
All that I hope for 'tis of thee.

Love American style,
Truer than the red, white and blue.
Love American style, Truer than the
    red white and blue (fade)

15

The Love Boat

THE SHOW: Take a luxury cruise liner, fill it with love-starved celebrities, and what do you have? *The Love Boat*, TV's first floating singles bar. The action is hot and heavy on the deck of the Pacific Princess, with weekly guest stars (Carol Channing, Raymond Burr, etc.) falling in and out and in and out of love as they head for exotic ports all over the world. At the helm of the ship: fatherly Captain Stubing, patrolling his lively domain to make sure that everyone plays by the rules, and occasionally getting bitten by the love bug himself. In fact, the whole crew seems to plunge in with shipboard romances whenever they get the chance. But somehow sitcoms never seem to change. Even with all the cabin-hopping, it all comes off as good clean fun, and the Love Boat keeps sailing along.

Gavin MacLeod stars as Captain Stubing in one of America's most popular sitcoms ever

THE SONG: Performed by Jack ("Dear Heart") Jones, it was released at least twice as a single, but missed the Top 40. Written by Paul Williams, who authored "We've Only Just Begun," "Just an Old-Fashioned Love Song," etc.

Main Cast

Capt. Merrill Stubing: Gavin MacLeod
Vicki Stubing (his daughter): Jill Whelan
Burl "Gopher" Smith (Yeoman-Purser): Fred Grandy
Dr. Adam Bricker (ship's physician): Bernie Koppell
Isaac Washington (bartender): Ted Lange
Julie McCoy (cruise director, 1977-84): Lauren Tewes
Judy McCoy (cruise director, 1984 -): Pat Klous
"Ace" Evans (photographer): Ted McGinley

Vital Statistics

Hour-long sitcom. ABC. Current.
First aired: Sept. 24, 1977
Most popular time slot: Saturday, 9:00-10:00 PM
Last show: Still in first run.
Ranked in a year's Top 25: 1978 (14); 1979 (17); 1980 (24); 1981 (5); 1982 (14); 1983 (9); 1984 (12)

INSIDE FACTS

BACKGROUND INFO:
• *The Love Boat* was adapted from a novel called *The Love Boats*.
• The book was written by a former cruise hostess named Jeraldine Saunders, who based the story on her real-life experiences.
• Three pilot films were made before the idea was sold as a series. They aired as TV movies during the 1976-77 TV season.
• It has always been filmed on a real cruise ship, with passengers acting as extras.
• Before *Love Boat's* premiere, it was difficult to get passengers to cooperate; they complained that the crew was in their way. This changed as soon as people began seeing themselves on TV.
• Its format was inspired by ABC's successful multi-story sitcom, *Love American Style*.

TRIVIA QUIZ

1. What are the "Love Boat Follies"?
2. Most of the episodes of *Love Boat* were filmed on two real cruise ships. One is the Pacific Princess. What's the other one?
3. Who played Marshall, Captain Stubing's brother?
4. For a sitcom character, what's unusual about Stubing's daughter Vicki?
5. *Love Boat* broke into the Top 20 in its first season, 1977-78. What was the #1 show that season?

ANSWERS
5. *Laverne and Shirley*
4. She's an illegitimate daughter
3. Gavin MacLeod
2. The Island Princess
1. A shipboard musical revue featuring the crew and big stars

The Love Boat

Words and Music by Charles Fox and Paul Williams

Love, exciting and new.
Come aboard, we're expecting you.

And love, life's sweetest reward,
let it float, it floats back to you.

The Love Boat
Soon will be making another run.
The Love Boat
Promises something for everyone.
Set a course for adventure,
Your mind on a new romance.

17

And love won't hurt anymore
It's an open smile on a friendly shore.
It's love.
It's love.

The Odd Couple

THE SHOW: When Felix Unger's wife threw him out of their apartment, Felix had nowhere to go — except 1049 Park Ave., the home of Oscar Madison. It seemed logical; Felix and Oscar were childhood friends, and Oscar had been living alone since *his* wife had told him to leave. So Felix showed up at Oscar's door, ready to move in. "Can two divorced men," asked the show's announcer at the beginning of each episode, "share an apartment without driving each other crazy?" Not these two. Felix, a professional photographer, was a neatness nut; Oscar, a sportswriter for the *New York Herald*, was a slob. Felix liked good wine and opera; Oscar liked cheap beer and gambling. And on and on. They put up with each other for five years. Then Felix and ex-wife Gloria remarried, leaving Oscar to mess things up in peace.
THE SONG: Originally the movie theme, with lyrics by the author of "Call Me Irresponsible," "High Hopes," and dozens more.

Jack Klugman and Tony Randall, two of America's favorite comedians, teamed up in The Odd Couple

Main Cast

Felix Unger: Tony Randall
Oscar Madison: Jack Klugman
Officer Murray Grechner (a friend): Al Molinaro
Speed (a poker-friend): Gary Walberg
Vinnie (a poker-friend): Larry Gelman
Roy (a poker-friend): Ryan MacDonald
Dr. Nancy Cunningham: Joan Hotchkiss
Miriam Wellby (Felix's girlfriend): Elinor Donahue

Vital Statistics

Half-hour sitcom. ABC.
First aired: September 24, 1970
Most popular time slot: Friday 9:30 – 10:00 PM (1971-73, 1974)
Last show: July 4, 1975
Never ranked in a year's Top 25 shows.

INSIDE FACTS

ABOUT THE ODD COUPLE:
- While a struggling N.Y. actor, Jack Klugman shared a $14/month apartment with Charles Bronson.
- His first TV series was in the "Harris Against the World" segment of *90 Bristol Court* in 1964-5.
- With a 5-pack-a-day cigarette habit, he developed throat cancer in 1975. A successful operation that saved his career inspired him to play a doctor — Quincy — in 1976.
- Tony Randall studied at Northwestern University to "correct" his native Oklahoma accent.
- After studying acting in N.Y.C., he landed a role in *Mr. Peepers*, a popular sitcom of the early '50s.
- This led to films like *Pillow Talk* and *Lover Come Back*, starring Doris Day and Rock Hudson.

TRIVIA QUIZ

1. Whose experiences inspired Neil Simon to write the play?
2. In real life, how did Miriam Wellby get her name?
3. What role did Klugman's wife play in the series?
4. What were the Pigeon sisters' first names?
5. Who played Myrna Turner, Oscar's secretary?

ANSWERS

1. His brother's
2. She was played by Elinor Donahue who'd been on *Father Knows Best*. Robert Young, who'd been "Father," was currently starring as Marcus Welby. Tony Randall thought of it as a tribute to him
3. Oscar's ex-wife Blanche
4. Cecily and Gwen
5. Penny Marshall

The Odd Couple

Words: Sammy Cahn, Music: Neal Hefti

No matter where they go,
They are known as the couple.
They're never seen alone,
So they're known as the couple

As I've indicated
They are never quite separated,
They are peas in a pod.
Don't you think that it's odd?

Their habits, I confess,
None can guess with the couple.
If one says no it's yes,
More or less with the couple

But they're laugh-provoking
Yet they don't really know they're
joking.
Don't you find when love is blind
It's kind of odd!

19

(REPEAT ALL VERSES)

Don't you think it's odd?
Don't you think it's odd?
Don't you think it's odd?

The Munsters

THE SHOW: Every day is Halloween at 1313 Mockingbird Lane, home of the ghoulish Munster family. The father, Herman (who works in a funeral parlor), is a "dead ringer" for Frankenstein; his wife Lily is a friendly lady vampire; Eddie, their son, is a werewolf; and 378-year-old Grandpa is Count Dracula. Actually, despite appearances, they're just an average American sitcom family. Mom, for example, cooks them all breakfast in the morning — in a steaming cauldron. And everyone looks up to Dad (who's over seven feet tall and so strong that he walks through walls). And of course they have pets — a bat named Igor, a prehistoric creature called Spot, and a raven that keeps repeating "Nevermore." Only Marilyn, their pretty niece, looks and acts human. But the rest of the family thinks she's monstrous, of course!

Is it Frankenstein's monster? Nope — it's lovable Herman Munster!

THE SONG: An instrumental on the show, the lyrics were written by the Munsters' producer, Bob Mosher and sung only once — on a kids' record. Later, Butch Patrick recorded a rock version with new lyrics. Title: "Whatever Happened to Eddie?"

Main Cast

Herman Munster: Fred Gwynne
Lily Munster (his wife): Yvonne DeCarlo
Grandpa: Al Lewis
"Eddie" Munster (his son): Butch Patrick
Marilyn Munster (his niece): Beverly Owen, Pat Priest

Vital Statistics

Half-hour sitcom. CBS. 70 episodes
First aired: September 24, 1964
Most popular time slot: Thursday 7:30 – 8:00 PM
Last show: September 8, 1966
Ranked in a year's Top 25: 1965 (18)

INSIDE FACTS

ABOUT HERMAN'S COSTUME:

• It took 2 hours to transform the bony 6'5", 180 lb. Fred Gwynne into Herman.

• His face was covered with grease, balloon rubber, and yellow-green makeup (even though the show was filmed in black-and-white).

• To make him look massive, he was given pants stuffed with foam in the legs, a shrunken jacket stuffed with foam in the shoulders and arms (it buttoned in the back), and 10-lb. boots with built-in 5" heels.

• The boots were designed to make it hard for Gwynne to walk in them, so he'd naturally have a clumsy, "lurching" walk.

• The costume was so hot that at first, Gwynne lost 10 lbs. sweating in it.

TRIVIA QUIZ

THE SUBJECT IS . . . THE MUNSTERS

1. What was the name of the funeral home where Herman worked?
2. What kind of milk did the Munsters drink?
3. What was Eddie's dog's name?
4. In what town did the Munsters live?
5. Who played Dr. Dudley, the Munsters' physician (hint: he played Uncle Arthur on *Bewitched*)?

ANSWERS

1. Gateman, Goodbury, and Graves
2. Bat milk
3. Woof Woof
4. Mockingbird Heights
5. Paul Lynde

The Munsters Theme

Words: Robert Mosher, Music: Jack Marshall

1. When you are walk-ing the street at night, and be-hind you there's no-one in
2. If when you're sleep-ing you dream a lot, ghou-lish night-mares pa-rade thru your

view, but you hear mys-ter-i-ous feet at night, then the
head. And then you wake up and scream a lot, oh the

Mun-sters are fol-low-ing you. If you should meet this strange
Mun-sters are un-der your bed. At mid-night if crea-tures should

fa-mi-ly, just for-get what some peo-ple have said. The
prowl a-bout and if vam-pires and vul-tures swoop down and

21

M·A·S·H

THE SHOW: Although it was often hilariously funny, M*A*S*H didn't gloss over the horrors of war like other "war comedies." It took us right into the operating room, where doctors and nurses of the 4077th worked furiously to save the wounded — and sometimes failed. Located a few miles from the front lines during the Korean War, this army hospital frequently resembled a 3-ring circus. The ringmaster (and top surgeon): Hawkeye Pierce, a reluctant draftee whose constant one-liners made him a sort of Groucho Marx with a scalpel. The supporting cast included more than 20 people in the show's 11-year run — which, by the way, was about 4 times as long as the actual Korean War.

*M*A*S*H helped make Alan Alda one of America's most popular personalities*

THE SONG: Originally the movie theme. Lyrics were written by the director's son, and sung in the film when a character was contemplating suicide.

Main Cast

Capt. Hawkeye Pierce: Alan Alda
Capt. John McIntyre (Trapper John): Wayne Rogers
Maj. Margaret Houlihan (Hot Lips): Loretta Swit
Maj. Frank Burns: Larry Linville
Cpl. Walter O' Reilly (Radar): Gary Burghoff
Lt. Col. Henry Blake: McLean Stevenson
Father Francis Mulcahy: William Christopher
Cpl. Maxwell Klinger: Jamie Farr
Col. Sherman Potter: Harry Morgan
Capt. B. J. Hunnicut: Mike Farrell
Maj. Charles Emerson Winchester: David Ogden Stiers

Vital Statistics

Half-hour sitcom. CBS.
First aired: September 17, 1972
Most popular time slot: Tues. 9:00-9:30 PM (1975-78)
Mon. 9:00-9:30 PM (;1978-83)
Last show: September 19, 1983
Ranked in a year's Top 25: 1974 (4); 1975 (5) 1976 (15); 1977 (4); 1978 (9); 1979 (7); 1980 (5); 1981 (4); 1982 (9); 1983 (3)

INSIDE FACTS

BACKGROUND INFO:
- M*A*S*H originated as a novel written by Maine physician J. Richard Hornberger, using the pseudonym Richard Hooker.
- He didn't want his honest account of Korean War experiences to damage his professional standing, so he didn't reveal himself until after the show was a hit.
- He was amused that the story was considered anti-war, since he was a conservative Republican.
- In 1970, director Robert Altman made a movie out of the novel.
- It was a smash, winning an Oscar for best script.
- On TV, its first-year ratings were erratic; CBS almost cancelled it mid-season.
- Alan Alda's father didn't want him to be an actor — he wanted him to be a *doctor!*

TRIVIA QUIZ

1. What does M.A.S.H. stand for?
2. Which discharge (give the number) did Klinger keep trying to get?
3. Who was Hot Lips married to?
4. How far was Toledo, according to a sign in the M*A*S*H camp?
5. What was Hawkeye's native state?

ANSWERS

5. Maine
4. 6133 Miles
3. Lt. Col. Donald Penobscott
2. Section 8
1. Mobile Army Surgical Hospital

Song From M*A*S*H* (Suicide Is Painless)

Words and Music: Mike Altman and Johnny Mandel

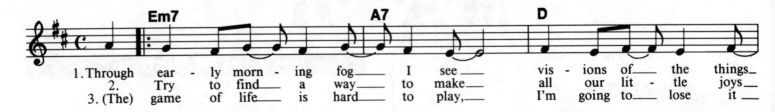

1. Through ear - ly morn - ing fog___ I see ___ vis - ions of ___ the things___
2. Try to find ___ a way ___ to make ___ all our lit - tle joys___
3. (The) game of life ___ is hard ___ to play, ___ I'm going to ___ lose it

24

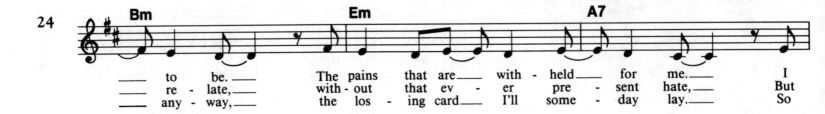

___ to be. ___ The pains that are ___ with - held ___ for me. ___ I
___ re - late, ___ with - out that ev - er pre - sent hate, ___ But
___ any - way, ___ the los - ing card ___ I'll some - day lay. ___ So

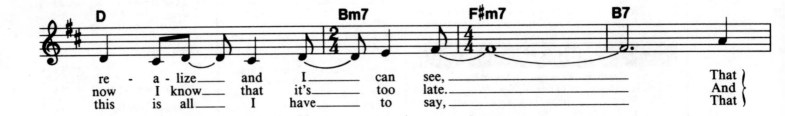

re - a - lize ___ and I ___ can see, _____ That
now I know ___ that it's ___ too late. _____ And
this is all ___ I have ___ to say, _____ That

CHORUS

Su - i - cide___ Is Pain - less, it brings on man - y chang -

- es, and I can take___ or leave___ it if___ I please___

1,2

3.

2. I
3. The

And you can do the

same thing if you please._____

25

The only way to win is cheat,
And lay it down before I'm beat,
And to another give a seat
For that's the only painless feat.
'Cause

26

CHORUS

Suicide is painless,
It brings on many changes,
And I can take or leave it
If I please

The sword of time will pierce our skins,
It doesn't hurt when it begins,
But as it works its way on in,
The pain grows stronger, watch it grin.
For   (CHORUS)

A brave man once requested me
To answer questions that are key,
Is it to be or not to be
And I replied "Oh, why ask me."
'Cause   (CHORUS)

AND NOW...

A Song From A Sponsor

Roto-Rooter

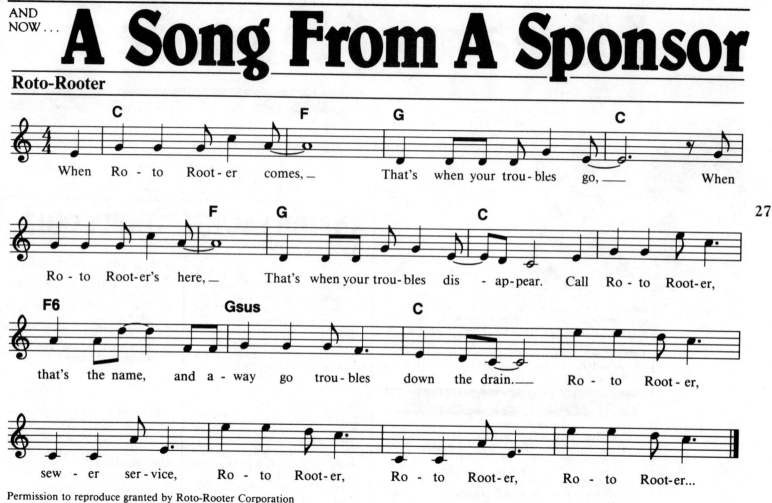

When Ro - to Root - er comes, — That's when your trou - bles go, — When
Ro - to Root - er's here, — That's when your trou - bles dis - ap-pear. Call Ro - to Root - er,
that's the name, and a - way go trou - bles down the drain.— Ro - to Root - er,
sew - er ser - vice, Ro - to Root - er, Ro - to Root - er, Ro - to Root - er...

I Dream of Jeannie

THE SHOW: Astronaut Tony Nelson seemed out of luck when his space mission aborted and he parachuted to a desert island ... until he uncorked an old bottle he'd found in the sand, releasing a beautiful genie named Jeannie. Grateful for her freedom, Jeannie granted Tony's wish to return to his home in Cocoa Beach, Florida. But that was just the beginning: Jeannie was so infatuated with her space hero that she decided to move in with him (just platonic, of course), turning his once-normal life into utter chaos. Only Tony's fellow-astronaut, Roger Healy, knew about Jeannie's magical powers (she could grant any wish with the blink of an eye). Everyone else thought he'd gone into orbit *permanently*. On Dec. 2, 1969, Jeannie got *her* wish when she and Tony were married. "Yes, master."

Larry Hagman and Barbara Eden, stars of I Dream of Jeannie

THE SONG: An instrumental on the show, but originally written with lyrics. Music by the composer of "The Good, the Bad, and the Ugly," "Hang 'Em High," and more.

Main Cast

Jeannie: Barbara Eden
Capt. Tony Nelson (her "Master"): Larry Hagman
Capt. Roger Healy (Tony's friend): Bill Daily
Dr. Alfred Bellows (psychiatrist): Hayden Rorke
Amanda Bellows (his wife): Emmaline Henry
Gen. Wingard Stone (1st C.O.): Philip Ober
Gen. Martin Peterson (2nd C.O.): Barton MacLane
Gen. Winfield Schaeffer (3rd C.O.): Vinton Hayworth

Vital Statistics

Half-hour sitcom. NBC. 139 episodes.
First aired: Sept. 18, 1965
Most popular time slot: Sat. 8:00-8:30 PM (1965-66),
Mon. 8:00-8:30 PM (1966-67),
Tues. 7:30-8:00 PM (1967-68)
Last show: Sept. 1, 1970
Never ranked in the Top 25 shows of a year.

INSIDE FACTS

ABOUT THE "NAVEL CONTROVERSY":
• Although network censors had no objection to Barbara Eden's sexy costume or the fact that Jeannie was living with a man for whom she would do anything (anything?), they *did* object to her navel showing.
• The solution: she had to put a flesh-colored cloth plug in it so it wouldn't show while filming. A milestone in censorship!

ABOUT JEANNIE:
• Her birthday: April 1, 64 B.C.
• How she wound up in a bottle: she was imprisoned by Blue Djin, the most powerful genie, when she refused to marry him (a truly sore loser).
• Her rescue date: Sept. 18, 1965. That would make her 2,029 years, 5 months, and 17 days old when she emerged from captivity.

TRIVIA QUIZ

1. How did Tony find the bottle in which Jeannie was imprisoned?
2. How was he rescued from the desert island?
3. How did Jeannie get back to Florida with Tony?
4. What was Jeannie's sister's name?
5. To what rank was Tony promoted late in the show?

ANSWERS

1. He was looking for something with which to send an SOS
2. Jeannie blinked him a rescue helicopter
3. She blinked herself back into the bottle, and sneaked into his survival kit
4. Jeannie II
5. Major

Jeannie   Words and Music by Buddy Kaye and Hugo Montenegro

eannie, fresh as a daisy,
Just look how she obeys me,
Does things that just amaze me so.

he smiles, presto the rain goes,
She blinks, out comes a rainbow,
Cars stop, even the train goes slow.

hen she goes by,
She makes sunshine on every rafter,
Sprinkles the air with laughter,
We're close as a quarter after three.

(There's no one like)
Jeannie, I'd introduce her
To you, but it's no use sir,
'Cause my Jeannie's in love with me.

She's in love with me!

Cheers

THE SHOW: Welcome to *Cheers,* America's favorite neighborhood bar. Pull up a stool, order yourself a drink, and relax. There are no celebrities here — just normal people with everyday problems. The owner/bartender is Sam Malone, a reformed alcoholic and former baseball player with the Boston Red Sox. His absent-minded old coach, Ernie Pantusso, used to help him out behind the bar. But Ernie passed away, leaving only Diane Chambers (Sam's ex-lover) and Carla Tortelli (with her houseful of kids) to wait on tables. Every week customers come and go at *Cheers,* but you can always count on seeing at least a few regulars whenever you drop in — usually wise-guy Norm, and Cliff, the mailman. *Cheers!*

Ted Danson, star of Cheers

THE SONG: Co-written and sung by Gary Portnoy, it was released as a single twice, in 1983 and 1984. In '83 it broke into the Top 100, but never became a hit. It is among the best-known themes of the '80s. Included by request.

Main Cast

Sam Malone (Cheers owner): Ted Danson
Diane Chambers (waitress): Shelly Long
Carla Tortelli (waitress): Rhea Perlman
Dr. Frasier Crane (Diane's fiance): Kelsey Grammer
"Coach" Pantusso (bartender): Nicholas Colasanto
Cliff Clavin (a patron): John Ratzenberger
Norm Peterson (a patron): George Wendt

Vital Statistics

Half-hour sitcom. NBC. Current.
First aired: Sept. 30, 1982
Most popular time slot: Thursday, 9:00-9:30 PM
Last show: Still in first run.

INSIDE FACTS

MISCELLANEOUS:
● *Cheers* was inspired by a real Boston bar named the "Bull and Finch."
● The show was created by the writers and producers of *Taxi.*
● Most of the cast were TV newcomers. Only George Wendt and Rhea Perlman had appeared in network sitcoms — Wendt in the short-lived *Making The Grade,* and Perlman in an occasional *Taxi.*
● Ted Danson got his start on TV in the soap opera *Somerset* in the '70s.
● Despite critical raves, *Cheers* received low ratings at first. NBC renewed it anyway.
● It went on to win an impressive batch of Emmy Awards, including Best Comedy Program, Best Actress, Best Script, Best Director, etc.

TRIVIA QUIZ

**THE SUBJECT IS . . .
TV HANGOUTS**
Cheers is the name of a bar and a hang-out. Name the shows associated with these other hang-outs:
1. Kelsey's Bar
2. Arnold's Drive-In
3. The Pizza Bowl
4. Mel's Diner
5. The Longbranch Saloon

ANSWERS
1. *All In the Family*
2. *Happy Days*
3. *Laverne and Shirley*
4. *Alice*
5. *Gunsmoke*

Cheers (Where Everybody Knows Your Name)

Words and Music by Gary Portnoy and Judy Hart

Making your way in the world today
Takes everything you've got.
Taking a break from all your worries
Sure would help a lot.
Wouldn't you like to get away?

Chorus:

Sometimes you wanna go
Where everybody knows your name.
And they're always glad you came.
You wanna be where you can see
Our troubles are all the same.
You wanna be where everybody knows
   your name
You wanna go where people know
People are all the same.
You wanna go where everybody knows
   your name.

Climbing the walls when no one calls;
You've lost at love again.
And the more you're down and out,
The more you need a friend
When you long to hear a kind hello.

CHORUS

Gilligan's Island

THE SHOW: Skipper Jonas Grumby (you didn't know he had a name, did you?) and his sidekick, Gilligan, set sail on the SS Minnow with a weird assortment of passengers: Thurston Howell III and his wife (wealthy snobs), Ginger Grant (a glamourous movie star), Roy Hinkley (a research scientist), and Mary Ann Summers (the girl-next-door). It was only supposed to be a three-hour tour. But then the weather started getting rough, the ship was tossed, and . . . well, you know the rest. Gilligan and the gang were shipwrecked on a tiny uncharted island in the South Pacific for three whole seasons. There were lots of visitors, from cosmonauts to surfers, but somehow the cast never managed to escape. But the real mystery was: why did they pack all that luggage for a three-hour tour?

One of the funniest TV comedians of the '60s — Bob Denver

THE SONG: CBS thought viewers wouldn't understand what 7 people were doing on an island every week, and wanted the show to be about a charter boat instead. Producer Sherwood Schwartz's solution: this song.

Main Cast

Gilligan: Bob Denver
Jonas Grumby (the Skipper): Alan Hale
Ginger Grant (the movie star): Tina Louise
Mary Ann Summers: Dawn Wells
Roy Hinkley (the professor): Russell Johnson
Thurston Howell III (the millionaire): Jim Backus
Lovey Howell III (his wife): Natalie Schafer

Vital Statistics

Half-hour sitcom. CBS. 98 episodes.
First aired: Sept. 26, 1964
Most popular time slot: Saturday, 8:30-9:00 PM (1964-65)
Last show: Sept. 4, 1967
Ranked in a year's Top 25: 1965 (19); 1966 (22)

INSIDE FACTS

BACKGROUND INFO:

- It was inspired by Daniel Defoe's *Robinson Crusoe*.
- The name Gilligan was picked out of the Los Angeles phone book.
- Creator Sherwood Schwartz, who had a degree in psychology, wanted to create a microcosm of American society on the island.
- Each of the 7 characters was supposed to represent a segment of society: "a glamour girl, a country girl, an intellectual, a misfit, a resourceful bull of a man, and a wealthy couple."
- The pilot was filmed in six days on a Hawaiian island, at a cost of $175,000.
- CBS rejected the original pilot. Schwartz then re-edited it, adding a theme song that explained what they were doing on the island. That sold it.

TRIVIA QUIZ

1. What did Mary Ann do for a living before she was ship-wrecked?
2. Where did Gilligan sleep?
3. Gilligan's favorite rock group once landed on the island. What were they called?
4. What did the Skipper do to Gilligan when he got mad at him?
5. What was the Skipper's pet name for Gilligan?

ANSWERS

1. She was a clerk in a country store in Horners Corners, Kansas
2. In a hammock
3. The Mosquitoes
4. Hit him with his hat
5. "Little buddy"

The Ballad of Gilligan's Isle

By Sherwood Schwartz and George Wyle

Just sit right back and you'll hear a tale,
A tale of a fateful trip
That started from this tropic port
Aboard this tiny ship.

The mate was a mighty sailin' man,
The skipper brave and sure,
Five passengers set sail that day
For a three hour tour,
A three hour tour.

The weather started getting rough,
The tiny ship was tossed,
If not for the courage of the fearless crew,
The Minnow would be lost.
The Minnow would be lost.

The ship's aground on the shore of this
Uncharted desert isle,
With Gilligan,
The Skipper too,
The millionaire and his wife,
The movie star
And the rest
Are here on Gilligan's Isle

OR

The ship's aground on the shore of this
Uncharted desert isle,
With Gilligan,
The Skipper too,
The millionaire and his wife,
The movie star,
The professor and Mary Ann
Are here on Gilligan's Isle.

(*Note:* this ending was added later)

Father Knows Best

THE SHOW: Jim and Margaret Anderson and their three kids — "Princess," "Bud," and "Kitten" — were the classic American sitcom family of the 1950s. They lived at 607 South Maple Street in Springfield, U.S.A., where everything was as pure — and white — as *Ivory Soap*. Mom was the homemaker, Dad (a good-natured insurance agent) was the bread-winner, and the younger Andersons were all basically nice kids. They sometimes found themselves in trouble (nothing serious, of course), but their problems were just part of Growing Up, and provided great opportunities for Dad to show the

In the '50s, everyone wished they had a father like Robert Young.

world how understanding he was. After all, he *did* know best. This scenario may seem a little far-fetched today, but at the time it seemed Right . . . and for seven seasons we secretly wondered why *our* families weren't perfect too.
THE SONG: An instrumental that played while the family made its appearance. These are the lyrics originally written for it. "Margaret, I'm home."

Main Cast

Jim Anderson: Robert Young
Margaret Anderson (his wife): Jane Wyatt
Betty Anderson (his daughter): Elinor Donahue
Bud Anderson (his son): Billy Gray
Kathy Anderson (his daughter): Lauren Chapin
Ed Davis (a neighbor): Robert Foulk
Myrtle Davis (his wife): Vivi Jannia

Vital Statistics

Half-hour sitcom. CBS. NBC. ABC. 203 episodes
First aired: October 3, 1954
Most popular time slots: Mon. 8:30–9:00 PM (1958-60),
Tues. 8:00–8:30 PM (1960-61)
Last show: September 17, 1962
Ranked in a year's Top 25 1958 (25); 1959 (14); 1960 (6)

INSIDE FACTS

A QUICK HISTORY:

● It debuted as a radio serial in 1949, on NBC.
● The radio show — also featuring Robert Young — was called *Father Knows Best?* The question mark was intentional.
● It's hard to believe, but after two years on CBS, the TV show was cancelled.
● Irate viewers flooded the nework with letters.
● The result: it was picked up by NBC for the following season, and aired at an earlier time so families could watch it together.
● At the height of the show's popularity, Robert Young decided he was tired of it, and quit.
● It was so popular that re-runs were shown in prime time for 3 more years.

TRIVIA QUIZ

1. What was Bud's real first name?
2. What insurance company did Jim Anderson manage?
3. When Betty and Bud each graduated from high school, where did they go to college?
4. In 1977, the cast got together again for *The Father Knows Best Reunion.* What was the occasion?
5. Elinor Donahue played "the girlfriend" in a '60s and a '70s sitcom. In one she was Ellie Walker, in the other Miriam Wellby. What shows?

ANSWERS

1. James Anderson, Jr.
2. The General Insurance Company
3. State College, in Springfield
4. The Andersons' 35th wedding anniversary
5. *The Andy Griffith Show,* and *The Odd Couple*

Waiting (Theme From "Father Knows Best")

Words: Leon Pober, Music: Don Ferris and Irving Friedman

Wait - ing_____ for love to find you_____ is

some - thing_____ worth wait - ing for_____

35

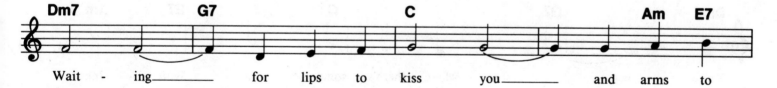

Wait - ing_____ for lips to kiss you_____ and arms to

hold you_____ for - ev - er - more._____ Oh,

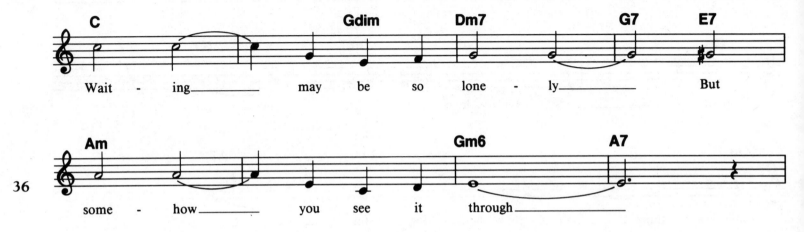

Wait - ing_____ may be so lone - ly_____ But

36

some - how_____ you see it through_____

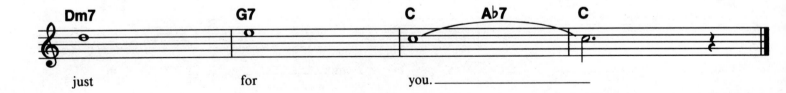

Know - ing_____ some - where there's some - one Wait - ing

just for you._____

Chico and the Man

THE SHOW: Chico and the Man were TV's *other* odd couple. Chico Rodriguez was a fast-talking, street-wise Chicano; Ed Brown was a cranky old garage-owner in the Barrio of East Los Angeles. Somehow, Chico convinced Ed to hire him as a mechanic, and he moved into an old beat-up truck in the garage. Ed lived there too, so there was bound to be trouble. But even though they always seemed to be fighting, the pair gradually grew closer. In fact, Chico ("Looking good!") became a second son to widower Ed. Things really *were* looking good for this top-rated comedy. Then, half-way through the third season, tragedy struck: Freddie Prinze took his own life. But despite the star's sudden death, the program carried on. Ed adopted a new "Chico" — 12-year-old Raul — who lasted until the series was cancelled.

Freddie Prinze played Chico

THE SONG: Performed by Jose Feliciano, who composed it during a twenty-minute car ride on his way to a meeting with the show's producers — the meeting in which he was supposed to present the song!

Main Cast

Ed Brown (the Man): Jack Albertson
Chico Rodriguez: Freddie Prinze
Louie (the garbage man): Scatman Crothers
Della Rogers (Ed's landlord): Della Reese
Raul (adopted by Ed): Gabriel Melgar
Mando (Chico's pal): Isaac Ruiz
Reverend Bemis: Ronnie Graham

Vital Statistics

Half-hour sitcom. NBC.
First aired: Sept. 13, 1974
Most popular time slot: Friday, 8:30-9:00 PM (1974-76)
Last show: July 21, 1978
Ranked in a year's Top 25: 1975 (3), 1976 (25)

INSIDE FACTS

ABOUT THE "CHICO" CONTROVERSY
- From the outset, there were problems.
- Mexican-American groups protested the use of the term "Chico," which means "boy." They called it demeaning.
- They said the dialogue was racist, and threatened a boycott of the sponsor's products (a sample: the Man to Chico: "Get out of here and take your flies with you").
- They said it was unfair to portray Prinze as a Mexican-American, since he was, in fact, of Puerto Rican and Hungarian ancestry.
- They even complained about the theme song, which is a flamenco-style tune, saying it had nothing to do with Mexican-American music.
- The show was altered to accommodate them, but the theme stayed.

TRIVIA QUIZ

THE SUBJECT IS ...
VIEWER PROTESTS
Chico sparked a protest in 1974 from irate viewers. Here are other TV viewer/network confrontations. Can you name them?

1. Jews and Catholics protested the mixed marriage in this 1972 sitcom
2. Mexican-Americans protested this sombrero-wearing animated ad character in the late '60s
3. When NBC cancelled this series in 1968, it received the most protest letters in its history
4. When ABC interrupted this show to announce the safe return of an imperiled astronaut, it got a flood of irate phone calls

ANSWERS

1. *Bridget Loves Bernie*
2. *The Frito Bandito*
3. *The Monkees*
4. *Batman*

Chico And The Man (Main Theme)

Words and Music: José Feliciano

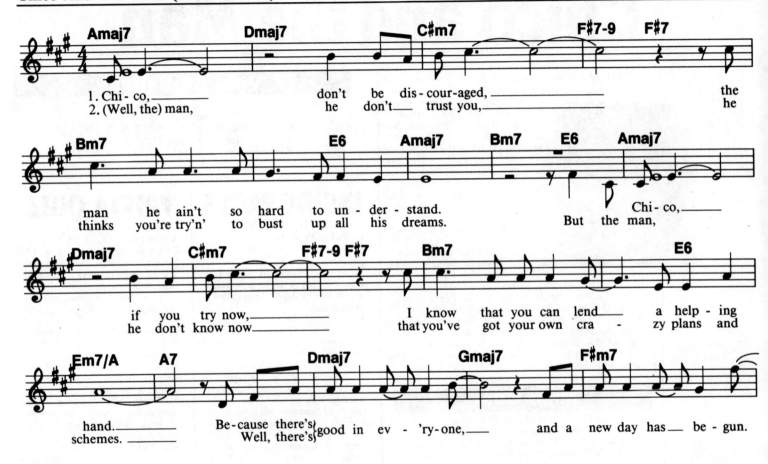

38

You can see the morn - ing sun___ if you try.___ And I know___ things will be bet-ter;___ {I know / Oh, yes} they will for Chi- co and___ the man.___ 2. Well, the Chi- co and___ the man;___ ___ yes they will___ for Chi - co and___ the man.___

39

Gidget

THE SHOW: "Everybody's goin' surfing, surfing USA." In the early '60s, surfing fever swept across America. But TV didn't catch the wave until 1965, by which time the Beatles had already overtaken the Beach Boys as trend-setters. TV's version: *Gidget*, a series about fun, fun, fun in the California sun. Like the popular movie, it chronicled the good-natured antics of Francine Lawrence (Gidget) and her surfer pals — Jeff Matthews (Moon Doggie), Siddo, Larue, and Treasure. Together, they frolicked on the shores of Santa Monica, playing Beach Blanket Bingo, hanging out, hanging ten, and watching assorted gremmies and hodads trying to shoot the curl. Parental guidance was provided by Gidget's father, Russell, an English professor. The show introduced future superstar Sally Field in the lead role, but wiped out after one year anyway.

Sally Field before her career really took off.

THE SONG: Recorded by Johnny Tillotsen, and co-written by Howard Greenfield, whose many credits include *Bewitched* and *Calendar Girl*.

Main Cast

Frances Lawrence (Gidget): Sally Field
Professor Russell Lawrence (her father): Don Porter
Anne Cooper (her sister): Betty Conner
John Cooper (her brother-in-law): Peter Deuel
Jeff Mathews (Moon Doggie): Steven Miles
Larue (Gidget's friend): Lynette Winter
Treasure (a friend): Beverly Adams
Siddo (a friend): Mike Nader

Vital Statistics

Half-hour sitcom. ABC. 32 episodes.
First aired: Sept. 15, 1965
Most popular time slot: Wednesday, 8:30-9:00 PM, Thurs. 8:00-8:30 PM
Last show: Sept. 1, 1966
Never ranked in the Top 25 shows of a year.

INSIDE FACTS
ABOUT GIDGET AND SURFING:

• There really was a surfer-girl known as Gidget (no joking).
• Her name was Kathy Kohner.
• She got her nickname from the other surfers. She explained: "I'm so small [they] called me 'Midget.' I got mad. So now it's Gidget. A girl midget. A gidget. Get it?"
• Her father, Frederick Kohner, wrote a book about her adventures, which was a best-seller in 1957.
• In 1959 it was adapted into a popular movie called *Gidget*, which gave surfing its first national exposure.
• In the film, Sandra Dee played the starring role.
• After she got the TV role, Sally Field revealed that she didn't know how to surf. She had to take lessons from surfer champion Darryl Stolper.

TRIVIA QUIZ
THE SUBJECT IS . . .
SALLY FIELD

Sally went from Gidget to other starring roles in film and TV. Name . . .
1. Her 2 Oscar-winning movies
2. Her convent name in *The Flying Nun*
3. The short-lived TV series in which she played a newlywed with E.S.P. (1973-74)
4. The film in which she co-starred with Burt Reynolds
5. The TV-movie for which she won an Emmy in 1977

ANSWERS

1. *Norma Rae, and Places in the Heart*
2. Sister Bertrille
3. *The Girl With Something Extra*
4. *Smokey and the Bandit*
5. *Sybil*

If you're in doubt about angels being
 real,
I can arrange to change any doubts you
 feel.
Wait 'til you see my Gidget,
You're headed for a big surprise.
The way she walks, the way she talks,
You won't believe your eyes.

No work of art can touch you
Like she'll touch your heart.
Everyone who sees her
Thereupon agrees her
Face can replace
The Mona Lisa.

If there's a phrase to praise her, it's hard
 to find.
Webster, indeed, would need a new
 book to bind.
Wait 'til you see my Gidget,
The dictionary's out of date.
Compared to her, the words that were,
are only second-rate.

She's got the smile and style that you
 can't resist,
The way she moves just proves angels
 do exist.
Wait 'til you see my Gidget,
You'll want her for your Valentine.
You're gonna say she's all that you
 adore,
But stay away, my Gidget is spoken for.
You're gonna find
That Gidget is mine.

41

The Partridge Family

THE SHOW: Gee whiz, those Partridges sure have a fun life, don't they? I mean, traveling around in their psychedelic bus, playing rock'n'roll all the time, just bein' stars. I'd give anything if I could do that! And anyway, their mom is so-o-o hip. My Mom wouldn't ever do what theirs does. I mean, wow, my Mom doesn't even know *how* to drive a bus, let alone sing in a rock band. And she's really uptight — not like Mrs. Partridge, who never really gets mad at the kids. She just kinda digs whatever's happening. You know, those guys sure got lucky when they made that record in their garage. I mean, to have a record company buy the song — and *then* to have it be a hit, too! I keep trying to get my brother to record us on his tape recorder, but he says he's too busy. Oh wow! Look, girls, like it's David Cassidy! He is *too* much! Isn't he dreamy? Far out! . . .

The Partridge Family catapulted David Cassidy to stardom

THE SONG: Sung by the Partridges while an animated egg cracked open and little birds paraded out.

Shirley Partridge: Shirley Jones
Keith Partridge: David Cassidy
Laurie Partridge: Susan Dey
Danny Partridge: Danny Bonaduce
Tracy Partridge: Suzanne Crough
Christopher Partridge: Jeremy Gelbwaks (1970-71), Brian Forster (1971-74)
Reuben Kinkaid (their manager): David Madden

Vital Statistics

Half-hour sitcom. ABC. 96 episodes.
First aired: Sept. 25, 1970
Most popular time slot: Friday, 8:30-9:00 (1970-73)
Last show: Aug. 31, 1974
Ranked in a year's Top 25: 1972 (16), 1973 (19)

INSIDE FACTS

THE PARTRIDGE CRAZE:
• They were described by a Screen Gems exec in 1972 as "the Partridge Family money machine."
• Their show, records, and licensed merchandise reportedly earned $11 million a year.
• Merchandise included bubble-gum cards, love beads, bumper stickers, astrological charts, lunch boxes, and lots more.
• A children's-wear manufacturer introduced a line of Partridge fashions.
• 200,000 people paid $2 each for membership in their fan club.
• *The Partridge Family Magazine* sold 400,000 copies a month.
• They sold millions of albums and had 7 Top 40 singles, in spite of the fact that none of them played on the records, and only David Cassidy and Shirley Jones even sang on them.

TRIVIA QUIZ

1. What did Shirley Jones have to learn to do for her role on the show?
2. What was the Partridges' dog named?
3. What was the Partridges' hometown in California?
4. What was Shirley Partridge's marital status?
5. The Partridge Family had 2 Top 10 hits besides "I Think I Love You." Name one

ANSWERS

1. Drive with a stick shift (to drive the bus)
2. Simone
3. San Pueblo — address (for fanatics): 698 Sycamore Road.
4. Widowed
5. "Doesn't Somebody Want To Be Wanted," (#6, 1971), "I'll Meet You Halfway" (#9, 1971)

Come On Get Happy (The Partridge Family Theme)

by Wes Farrell and Danny Janssen

Hello world, hear the song that we're
    singin',
Come on get happy.
A whole lot of lovin' is what we'll be
    bringin'.
We'll make you happy.

We had a dream we'd go travelin'
    together,
We'd spread a little lovin' then we'd
    keep movin' on.
Somethin' always happens whenever
    we're together,
We get a happy feelin when we're
    singin' a song.

Trav'lin' along there's a song that we're
    singin',
Come on get happy.
A whole lot of lovin' is what we'll be
    bringin',
We'll make you happy.
We'll make you happy.
We'll make you happy.

43

Rawhide

THE SHOW: While Marshal Matt Dillon was patrolling Dodge City, and Ben Cartwright was taking care of business at the Ponderosa, trail boss Gil Favor and his trusty ramrod, Rowdy Yates, were out on the trail eating dust. Their endless mission: get a herd of cattle (or "beeves," as the cowhands called 'em) from San Antonio, Texas, to Sedalia, Kansas. It was tough work — but then, these guys were tough *men.* For seven years they hardly ever stopped, except to eat (grub was provided by that classic chuckwagoneer, Wishbone) or to meet some interesting new character who'd

Keep them cameras rollin': Rawhide was Clint Eastwood's first starring role.

provide the story line for the week. Most of the time they kept "them dogies rollin'." An interesting sidelight: *Rawhide* was actually based on the 1860s experiences of a Texas trail boss, whose diaries provided the original inspiration for the show.

THE SONG: Sung by Frankie Laine, and written by the composers of *High Noon* and *When You Wish Upon A Star.* Reappeared as a dog food commercial in the '80s.

Main Cast

Gil Favor (the trail boss): Eric Fleming
Rowdy Yates (the ramrod): Clint Eastwood
Peter Nolan (the trail scout): Sheb Wooley
Wishbone (the cook): Paul Brineger
Hey Soos Patines (a drover): Robert Cabaj
Mushy (a drover): James Murdock

Vital Statistics

Hour-long western. CBS. 144 episodes.
First aired: Jan. 9, 1959
Most popular time slot: Friday, 7:30-8:30 PM
Last show: Jan. 4, 1966
Ranked in a year's Top 25: 1960 (18), 1961 (6), 1962 (13), 1963 (22)

INSIDE FACTS

CLINT EASTWOOD'S BIG BREAK:
• He had been "discovered" while he was working at a gas station in 1954 (he was also going to college).
• A screen test resulted in a Universal contract and several forgettable roles in forgettable movies.
• In 1956, he made his first TV appearance on *Highway Patrol.* He also made appearances on the syndicated *West Point* series.
• His big break came when, in 1958, he went to visit one of his wife's friends at CBS.
• While he was in the office, a CBS executive stopped in to visit the same friend.
• The executive knew that *Rawhide*'s producer was looking for an actor to play Rowdy, and, thinking Eastwood looked the part, invited him to read for it. He got the part. Instant star.

TRIVIA QUIZ

Clint Eastwood's role in *Rawhide* made him a star. Rowdy had a few pardners in that department — these 5 stars got "rollin'" as TV cowboys too. In what shows did they get their big breaks?
1. Steve McQueen
2. James Garner
3. Chuck Connors
4. Michael Landon
5. Lee Majors

ANSWERS

1. *Wanted: Dead or Alive*
2. *Maverick*
3. *The Rifleman*
4. *Bonanza*
5. *The Big Valley*

Rawhide

By Dimitri Tiomkin and Ned Washington

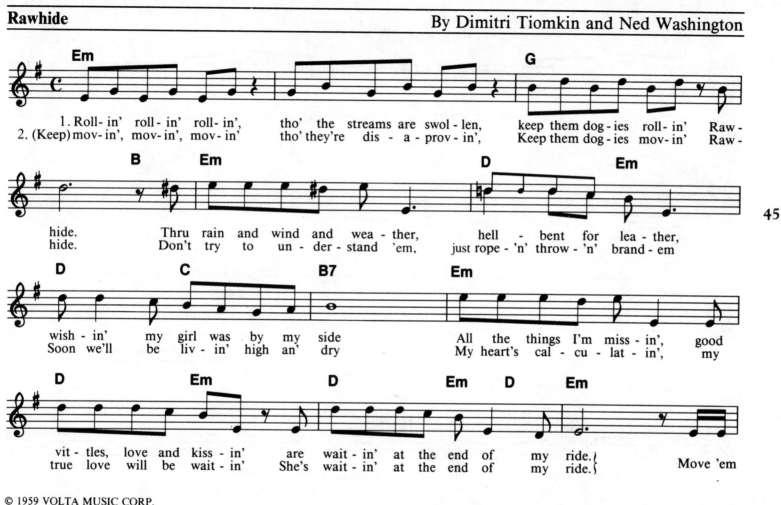

1. Roll- in' roll- in' roll- in', tho' the streams are swol- len, keep them dog- ies roll- in' Raw-
2. (Keep) mov- in', mov- in', mov- in' tho' they're dis- a- prov- in', Keep them dog- ies mov- in' Raw-

hide. Thru rain and wind and wea- ther, hell – bent for lea- ther,
hide. Don't try to un- der- stand 'em, just rope- 'n' throw- 'n' brand- em

wish- in' my girl was by my side All the things I'm miss- in', good
Soon we'll be liv- in' high an' dry My heart's cal- cu- lat- in', my

vit- tles, love and kiss- in' are wait- in' at the end of my ride.⎱
true love will be wait- in' She's wait- in' at the end of my ride.⎰

Move 'em

45

on, head 'em up, head 'em up, move 'em on, move 'em on, head 'em up, Raw - hide! Cut 'em

out! Tie 'em in! Ride 'em in! Turn 'em in! Cut 'em out! Ride 'em in, Raw -

hide. hide.

Ride 'em in! Raw - hide.

46

Sugarfoot

Will Hutchins starred as the bumbling cowboy, Sugarfoot.

THE SHOW: Tom Brewster was a peculiar western hero. He liked reading books, hated violence, and was terrible in gunfights (he could barely even shoot straight). In fact, he was so inept at traditional cowboy things that other cowboys had to invent a new term to describe him — "sugarfoot," one step lower than the lowly "tenderfoot." Brewster was an educated Easterner who was studying law with a correspondence school. He traveled west in the 1860s, full of dreams about the romance of the wild frontier, but kept finding trouble instead of adventure. And since he wasn't too handy with six-guns, all he could do was try to bluff his way out of dangerous situations. This method often flabbergasted his enemies. On the first episode of the show, for example, one villain (played by Dennis Hopper) asked him: "Whaddya tryin' to do, talk me to death?" And he was!

THE SONG: Sung by a chorus over the credits, it is one of the best-remembered western themes. Included by request.

Main Cast

Tom Brewster (Sugarfoot): Will Hutchins

Vital Statistics

Hour-long western. ABC.
First aired: September 17, 1957
Most popular time slot: Tuesday 7:30 – 8:30 PM (1957-59)
Last show: July 3, 1961
Ranked in a year's Top 25: 1958 (24); 1959 (21)

INSIDE FACTS
ABOUT SUGARFOOT'S CRAZY SCHEDULE:

● Although it was in the Top 25 twice, *Sugarfoot* never aired as a weekly series. In fact, you never knew what you'd see in its scheduled time slot.

● In its first year, it alternated each week with *Cheyenne*, starring Clint Walker as Cheyenne Bodie.

● In the middle of the second year, Walker left *Cheyenne* and was replaced by Ty Hardin as Bronco Layne. But the show was still called *Cheyenne*, and it still alternated with *Sugarfoot.*

● In 1959, Walker returned and *Bronco* became a separate series. Now *Cheyenne* alternated with *Shirley Temple,* and *Bronco* switched off with *Sugarfoot.*

● In 1960, *Sugarfoot*'s last year, *Cheyenne, Bronco,* and *Sugarfoot* rotated in the same time slot.

TRIVIA QUIZ
THE SUBJECT IS...
NAMES

Sugarfoot was one of many westerns whose title was the name of its main character. Here are 5 more. Name them.
1. A 6′7″ half-breed drifter
2. A Pappy-quoting gambler
3. An ex-Confederate Army captain roaming the west
4. A New Orleans gambler/adventurer who used a little gun. His protection was Pahoo
5. He wore a derby hat, and carried a cane

ANSWERS

1. *Cheyenne* (Cheyenne Bodie)
2. *Maverick* (Bret and Bart Maverick)
3. *Bronco* (Bronco Layne)
4. *Yancy Derringer*
5. *Bat Masterson*

Sugarfoot

Words: Paul Francis Webster, Music: Ray Heindorf and Max Steiner

Sug - ar - foot, Sug - ar - foot, eas - y lop - in', cat - tle rop - in' Sug - ar - foot,

Care - free as the tum - ble - weeds, a - jog - gin' a - long with a heart full of song And a

ri - fle and a vol - ume of the law. Sug - ar - foot, Sug - ar - foot,

nev - er un - der - es - ti - mate a Sug - ar - foot, Once you get his dan - der up, ain't

48

no one who's quick - er on the draw. You'll find him,_____ on the side of law and

or - der,_____ From the Mex - i - cal - i bor - der,_____ to the roll - ing hills of **49**

Ar - kan - saw; Sug - ar - foot, Sug - ar - foot, eas - y lop - in', cat - tle rop - in'

Sug - ar - foot, Rid - in' down to cat - tle - town, a - jog - gin' a - long with a

heart full of song And a ri - fle and a vol - ume of the law._____

The Rebel

THE SHOW: Johnny Yuma, the angry young man with the Confederate Army cap perched on his head, "roamed through the west" after the Civil War. Just what he did there every Sunday night for two years is hard to recall. But presumably it was the standard western stuff — save ranchers threatened by bad guys, save women threatened by bad guys, save towns threatened by bad guys...you know. Actually, there *was* something a little different about this program: it was the first western to show that post-Civil War Americans were confused and angry. Johnny, described by one critic as

Nick Adams as Johnny Yuma, The Rebel.

"TV's first truly tragic hero," was plunged into an identity crisis by the South's humiliating defeat. As he made the rounds of the western settlements, he seemed to be looking for something — a place to settle down, a meaning to life, some peace of mind. No kidding! Apparently, there was no market for even a quasi-philosophical western, as *The Rebel* quickly disappeared. Great song, though.

THE SONG: Johnny Cash's first TV theme. Released as a single, it became a Top 20 Country/Western hit in 1961.

Main Cast

Johnny Yuma: Nick Adams

Vital Statistics

Half-hour western. ABC. 76 episodes.
First aired: October 4, 1959
Most popular time slot: Sunday 9:00 – 9:30 PM (1959-61)
Last show: September 24, 1961
Never ranked in a year's Top 25 shows.

INSIDE FACTS

ABOUT NICK ADAMS:
• This show was the second important "Rebel" in his career.
• The first was his screen debut in *Rebel Without A Cause*; he played a member of the gang that was out to get James Dean (Dennis Hopper was also in the gang).
• After *The Rebel*, Adams played another soul-searching character on a series called *Saints and Sinners* (1962-63).
• He portrayed a crusading newspaper reporter for the *New York Bulletin* named Nick Alexander.

MISCELLANEOUS:
• *The Rebel* was co-produced by Mark Goodson-Bill Todman Productions (*The Price Is Right*, *Family Feud*, etc.)
• It was one of the few shows they had ever handled that was not a game show.

TRIVIA QUIZ

THE SUBJECT IS...1959
The Rebel debuted in the 1959-1960 TV season. Can you name the Top 5 shows in that season?
1. Matt Dillon had the #1 show
2. Ward Bond kept the settlers headed west in the #2 show
3. Richard Boone starred as Paladin in the year's #3 show
4. A comedian with a big nose co-starred with Marjorie Lord in the family sitcom that was #4
5. Freddie the Freeloader made frequent appearances in the year's #5 show

ANSWERS
1. Gunsmoke
2. Wagon Train
3. Have Gun, Will Travel
4. The Danny Thomas Show
5. The Red Skelton Show

The Rebel

Words and Music by Richard Markowitz and Andrew Fenady

Chorus:
Johnny Yuma was a rebel,
He roamed through the west,
Did Johnny Yuma THE REBEL,
He wander'd alone.

He searched the lands,
This restless lad,
He was panther quick and leather
  tough,
And he figured he'd been pushed
  enough,
THE REBEL, Johnny Yuma

CHORUS

He got fightin' mad
This rebel lad,
He packed no star as he wander'd far
When the only law was a hook and a
  draw,
THE REBEL, Johnny Yuma

CHORUS

He was fightin' mad,
This rebel lad,
With a dream he'd hold till his dying
  breath.
He'd search his soul and gamble with
  death,
THE REBEL, Johnny Yuma

CHORUS

The Lawman

THE SHOW: *The Lawman* was a product of the same TV factory that churned out *Cheyenne, Maverick, Bronco,* and *Sugarfoot* at the height of America's TV western craze in the late 1950s. Though not as well-remembered as its stable-mates today, it was surprisingly popular in its time (perhaps that's because it immediately followed *Maverick* on Sunday nights). The hero of the show was granite-jawed Dan Troop, U.S. Marshal in Laramie, Wyoming — a typical lawless frontier town. And the action was straight cowboy cops'n'robbers, with Troop and his trusty deputy Johnny McKay taking on bandits, rustlers and generic No-good Desperadoes. But the coolest things about Dan Troop were his neatly-trimmed mustache and his string tie. Viewers knew that any Marshal with that much style had to be indestructible; only the ratings could do *him* in.

THE SONG: Co-written by the team responsible for the themes from *77 Sunset Strip, Hawaiian Eye, Casper the Friendly Ghost,* and more. Immortal to those who watched the show, and one of the author's favorites.

John Russell played Marshal Dan Troop in The Lawman

Main Cast

Marshall Dan Troop: John Russell
Deputy Johnny McKay: Peter Brown
Lily Merrill (saloon owner): Peggie Castle
Jake (bartender): Dan Sheridan
Dru Lemp (cafe-owner): Bek Nelson

Vital Statistics

Half-hour western. ABC. 156 episodes.
First aired: October 5, 1958
Most popular time slot: Sunday 8:30 – 9:00 PM (1958-62)
Last show: October 9, 1962
Ranked in a year's Top 25: 1960 (15)

INSIDE FACTS

ABOUT THE STARS:
- John Russell starred in two other prime-time series besides *The Lawman.*
- His first role was in the 1955 syndicated show, *Soldiers of Fortune.* He played Tim Kelly, a mercenary adventurer.
- This show did so well that it attracted the attention of Warner Bros., which signed him up for *Lawman.*
- Six years after *Lawman* ended, he landed a role on the Robert Wagner series, *It Takes A Thief,* as Agent Dover.
- Peter Brown's next major TV role was on *Laredo.*
- It was a western that ran from 1965-67 on NBC. He played a Texas Ranger.
- Today, Brown is best known for his portrayal of Dr. Greg Peters in the soap opera, *Days of Our Lives.*

TRIVIA QUIZ

THE SUBJECT IS ...
LAWMEN
Like John Russell, these actors played classic western lawmen on TV. Name them:
1. James Arness (1955-75)
2. Henry Fonda (1959-61)
3. Hugh O'Brian (1955-61)
4. Gene Barry (1959-61)
5. Ray Teal (1959-73)

ANSWERS
1. Matt Dillon (*Gunsmoke*)
2. Marshal Simon Fry (*The Deputy*)
3. Wyatt Earp
4. Bat Masterson
5. Sheriff Roy Coffee (*Bonanza*)

Lawman (From the Warner Bros. series "LAWMAN")

Words: Mack David, Music: Jerry Livingston

The Law-man came with the sun, There was a job to be done,

And so they sent for the badge and the gun of the Law-man,_____ 53

_____ Law-man,_____ And as he si-lent-ly rode

Where e-vil vi-o-lent-ly flowed, They knew he'd live or he'd die by the

code of the Law-man,_____ Law-man._____

AND NOW...

A Song From A Sponsor

Brylcreem, A Little Dab'll Do Ya

Written by John P. Atherton

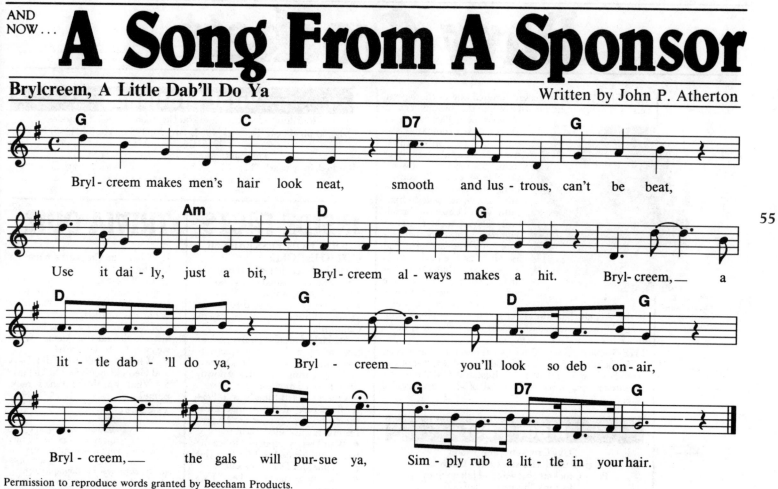

Bryl-creem makes men's hair look neat, smooth and lus-trous, can't be beat,

Use it dai-ly, just a bit, Bryl-creem al-ways makes a hit. Bryl-creem,— a

lit-tle dab-'ll do ya, Bryl-creem— you'll look so deb-on-air,

Bryl-creem,— the gals will pur-sue ya, Sim-ply rub a lit-tle in your hair.

55

Davy Crockett

THE SHOW: *Davy Crockett* inspired one of the biggest fads of the 1950s; in a matter of months, merchants sold millions of dollars worth of *Davy Crockett* coonskin caps, bubble gum cards, rifles, fringed jackets, and other items. Its popularity was incredible — especially considering the show never even aired as a regular series! Originally Walt Disney had broadcast "Davy Crockett, Indian Fighter " as just another feature on *Disneyland*. He had no idea that the public would respond so enthusiastically — in fact, the final episode of the scheduled 3-part adventure, in which Crockett was killed at the Alamo, had already been filmed. To satisfy audiences, Disney resurrected Crockett for a few more episodes about his early days as a frontiersman.

Actor/singer Fess Parker without his coonskin cap

THE SONG: A Top 20 hit four times in the same year, 1955! Parker's version hit #5, Bill Hayes' #1, Tennessee Ernie Ford's #5, and Walter Schuman's #14. An unprecedented record. It has 20 verses, all of which are included here.

Main Cast

Davy Crockett: Fess Parker
Georgie Russel (his sidekick): Buddy Ebsen
Polly Crockett (his wife): Helene Stanley
Mike Fink (his rival): Jeff York

Vital Statistics

Hour-long adventure, aired on *Disneyland*. ABC. 5 episodes.
Original air dates: Dec. 15, 1954; Jan. 26, 1955; Feb. 23, 1955; Nov. 16, 1955; Dec. 14, 1955
Time slot: Wednesday, 7:30 – 8:30 PM
Ranked in a year's Top 25: During original broadcast years, *Disneyland* ranked #6 (1954-55) and #4 (1955-56)

INSIDE FACTS

ABOUT HOW FESS PARKER GOT THE ROLE:
- He had decided to become an actor when he visited Hollywood in 1943 (while he was in the Navy).
- After WW II, he studied drama at the University of Southern California.
- He kicked around Hollywood for five years, making guest appearances on TV shows like *Dragnet*, and appearing in little-known, little-noticed movies.
- One of his B-films was a 1954 sci-fi feature about strange creatures who pop up near the Mojave Desert. It was called *Them*.
- Walt Disney happened to see the film, and decided to hire Fess (his real name) for *Davy Crockett*.
- The show made Parker "TV's first genuine overnight star."

TRIVIA QUIZ

1. What was Crockett's name for his rifle?
2. In 1962-63, Parker starred as Eugene Smith in a sitcom adaptation of a 1939 James Stewart film. What was it called?
3. Davy Crockett was the last man alive to defend the Alamo. What weapon was he left with?
4. What "bullet" trick did Davy and Georgie use to fool Mike Fink?
5. What was Mike Fink's nickname?

ANSWERS

1. Betsy
2. *Mr. Smith Goes To Washington*
3. Out of bullets, he was using his rifle as a club
4. They made it seem like Davy could catch a bullet in his teeth
5. "The King of the River"

The Ballad Of Davy Crockett

Words: Tom Blackburn, Music: George Bruns

1. Born on a moun-tain top in Ten - nes-see, Green - est state in the Land of the Free, Raised in the woods so's he knew ev - 'ry tree, kilt him a b'ar when he was on - ly three. Da - vy, Da - vy Crock-ett, King of the wild fron - tier! 2. In

2. (In) eigh - teen - thir - teen the Creeks up - rose, add - in' red-skin ar - rows to the coun - try's woes. Now, In - jun fight - in' is some - thin' he knows, so he should - ers his ri - fle an' off he___ goes. Da - vy, Da - vy Crock-ett, the man who don't know fear!

3. Off through the woods he's a - march - in' a - long, mak - in' up yarns an' a sing - in' a song, itch - in' fer fight - in' an' right - in' a wrong. He's ring - y as a b'ar an' twict as___ strong. Da - vy, Da - vy Crock-ett, the buck - skin buc - ca - neer!

57

4. **A**ndy Jackson is our gen'ral's name,
His reg'lar soldiers we'll put to shame,
Them redskin varmints us Volunteers'll tame,
'Cause we got the guns with the sure-fire aim.
Davy — Davy Crockett,
The champion of us all!

5. **H**eaded back to war from the ol' home place,
But Red Stick was leadin' a merry chase,
Fightin' an' burnin' at a devil's pace
South to the swamps on the Florida Trace.
Davy — Davy Crockett,
Trackin' the redskins down!

6. **F**ought single-handed through the Injun War
Till the Creeks was whipped an' peace was in store,
An' while he was handlin' this risky chore,
Made hisself a legend for evermore.
Davy — Davy Crockett,
King of the wild frontier!

7. **H**e give his word an' he give his hand
That his Injun friends could keep their land,
An' the rest of his life he took the stand
That justice was due every redskin band.
Davy — Davy Crockett.
Holdin' his promise dear!

8. **H**ome fer the winter with his family,
Happy as squirrels in the ol' gum tree,
Bein' the father he wanted to be,
Close to his boys as the pod an' the pea.
Davy — Davy Crockett,
Holdin' his young 'uns dear!

9. **B**ut the ice went out an' the warm winds came
An' the meltin' snow showed tracks of game,
An' the flowers of spring filled with woods with flame,
An' all of a sudden life got too tame.
Davy — Davy Crockett,
Headin' on West again!

10. **O**ff through the woods we're ridin' along,
Making' up yarns an' singin' a song,
He's ringy as a b'ar an' twict as strong,
An' knows he's right 'cause he ain't often wrong.
Davy — Davy Crockett,
The man who don't know fear!

11. **L**ookin' fer a place where the air smells clean,
Where the trees is tall an' the grass is green,
Where the fish is fat in an untouched stream,
An' the teemin' woods is a hunter's dream.
Davy — Davy Crockett,
Lookin' fer Paradise!

12. **N**ow he'd lost his love an' his grief was gall,
In his heart he wanted to leave it all,
An' lost himself in the forests tall,
But he answered instead his country's call.
Davy — Davy Crockett,
Beginnin' his campaign!

13. **N**eedin' his help they didn't
vote blind,
They put in Davy 'cause he
was their kind,
Sent up to Nashville the best
they could find,
A fightin' spirit an' a thinkin'
mind.
Davy — Davy Crockett,
Choice of the whole frontier!

14. **T**he votes were counted an' he
won hands down,
So they sent him off to
Washin'ton town
With his best dress suit still his
buckskins brown,
A livin' legend of growin'
renown.
Davy — Davy Crockett,
The Canebrake
Congressman!

15. **H**e went off to Congress an'
served a spell,
Fixin' up the Gover'ment an'
laws as well,
Took over Washin'ton so we
heered tell
An' patched up the crack in
the Liberty Bell.
Davy — Davy Crockett,
Seein' his duty clear!

16. **H**im an' his jokes travelled all
through the land,
An' his speeches made him
friends to beat the band,
His politickin' was their
favorite brand
An' everyone wanted to shake
his hand.
Davy — Davy Crockett,
Helpin his legend grow!

17. **H**e knew when he spoke he
sounded the knell
Of his hopes for White House
an' fame as well,
But he spoke out strong so
hist'ry books tell
An' patched up the crack in
the Liberty Bell.
Davy — Davy Crockett,
Seein' his duty clear!

18. **W**hen he come home, his
politickin' done,
The western march had just
begun,
So he packed his gear and his
trusty gun,
And lit out grinnin' to follow
the sun.
Davy — Davy Crockett,
Leadin' the pioneer!

19. **H**e heard of Houston an' Austin
an' so,
To the Texas plains he jest
had to go,
Where freedom was fightin'
another foe,
An' they needed him at the
Alamo.
Davy — Davy Crockett,
The man who don't know
fear!

20. **H**is land is biggest an' his land is
best,
From grassy plains to the
mountain crest,
He's ahead of us all, meetin'
the test,
Followin' his legend into the
West.
Davy — Davy Crockett,
King of the Wild Frontier!

59

The Carol Burnett Show

THE SHOW: Carol Burnett is one of the great comediennes in TV history. For 11 seasons (incredible, isn't it?)

The inimitable Carol Burnett

she hosted a one-hour variety series in which she sang, danced, and played a wide range of characters — from Queen Elizabeth to a rag-tag cleaning lady. Of course she had a little help from her friends every week. Her regular ensemble, Harvey Korman, Vicki Lawrence (who looked just like Carol), Lyle Waggoner, and Tim Conway worked together so smoothly that they set a new standard for TV variety shows. And they enjoyed themselves so much that they often burst out laughing in the middle of skits. Among the show's most popular features: "Ed and Eunice," the constantly bickering couple, and "As the Stomach Turns," a parody of soap operas. Every show opened with a question and answer period, and ended with Carol tugging on her ear.

THE SONG: Written especially as the show's closing theme by Carol's ex-husband and producer, Joe Hamilton.

Main Cast

Regular performers:

Carol Burnett	Tim Conway (1975-79)
Harvey Korman (1967-1977)	Dick Van Dyke (1977)
Lyle Waggoner (1967-1974)	Kenneth Mars (1979)
Vicki Lawrence (1967-79)	Craig Richard Nelson (1979)

Vital Statistics

Hour-long variety show. CBS.
First aired: Sept. 11, 1967
Most popular time slot: Monday, 10:00-11:00 (1967-71)
Last show: Sept. 8, 1979
Ranked in a year's Top 25: 1969 (24), 1970 (13), 1971 (25), 1972 (23), 1973 (22)

INSIDE FACTS

ABOUT CAROL'S CAREER:

• She became one of America's best known comediennes as a regular on *The Garry Moore Show*, from 1959-62.

• In her last year on the show, she won an Emmy for best performance in a music/variety series.

• After she left *Moore*, she tried her hand at films; her first movie: the forgettable *Who's Been Sleeping in My Bed*, with Dean Martin and Elizabeth Montgomery (1963).

• The next year, she hosted her first TV series. Called *The Entertainers*, it lasted less than one full season.

• *The Carol Burnett Show* ranks as the 8th-longest-running music/variety show in TV history, and the 3rd-longest show starring a woman (only Lucille Ball and Dinah Shore topped her).

TRIVIA QUIZ

Carol Burnett's supporting cast is almost as well-known as she is. Which one . . .
1. Was the bumbling Ensign Parker on *McHale's Navy*?
2. Had a #1 hit record the first time into a recording studio?
3. Starred in Mel Brooks' *Blazing Saddles*?
4. Co-starred in *Wonder Woman*?
5. Starred in the Broadway musical, *Bye Bye Birdie*?

ANSWERS

5. Dick Van Dyke
4. Lyle Waggoner
3. Harvey Korman
2. Vicki Lawrence (*The Night The Lights Went Out in Georgia*)
1. Tim Conway

It's Time To Say So Long

Words and Music: Joe Hamilton, Arranged by: Peter Matz

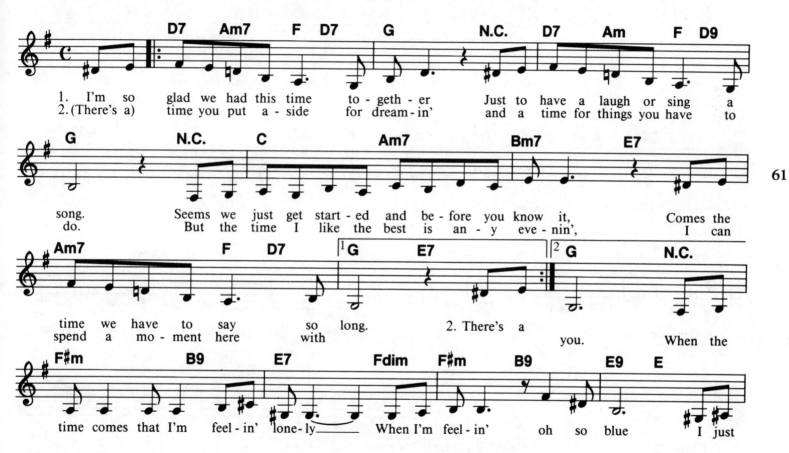

1. I'm so glad we had this time to-geth-er Just to have a laugh or sing a
2. (There's a) time you put a-side for dream-in' and a time for things you have to

song. Seems we just get start-ed and be-fore you know it, Comes the
do. But the time I like the best is an-y eve-nin', I can

time we have to say so long. 2. There's a
spend a mo-ment here with you. When the

time comes that I'm feel-in' lone-ly When I'm feel-in' oh so blue I just

61

A Song From A Sponsor

Rice-A-Roni

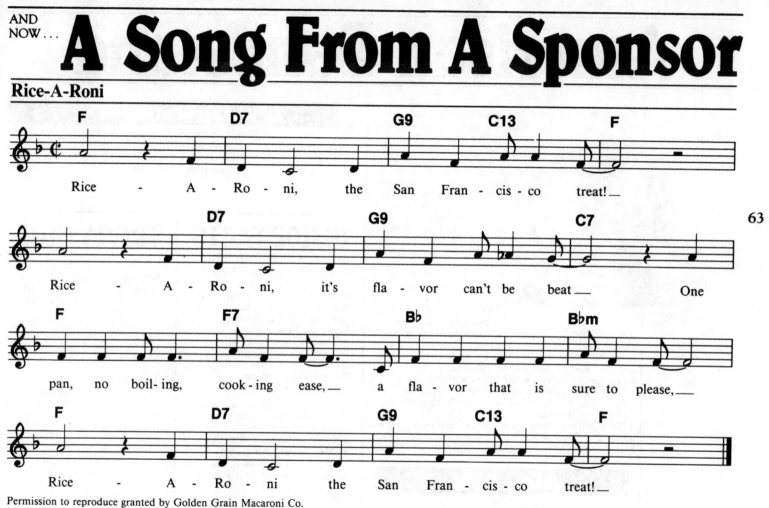

63

American Bandstand

THE SHOW: In 1956, a Philadelphia disc jockey took over as the host of a local TV rock'n'roll show called *Bandstand*. His name was Dick Clark. Before long, his popularity had attracted the attention of ABC-TV's home office, and the network decided to broadcast the show nationally as *American Bandstand*. It was a wise decision; almost three decades later, Clark has become one of the best-known personalities in TV history, and *Bandstand* has literally become an American institution (the Smithsonian has enshrined the podium Clark used). The most popular part of *Bandstand* was always the dancers, who became celebrities in their own right for awhile. But teenage viewers were also attracted by the stars who showed up to lip-sync their newest releases, and by "Rate-A-Record," in which a panel of judges (teenagers, of course) would rate new singles on a scale of 35-98. How could anyone help but give *American Bandstand* at *least* a 92? After all, it's always had a good beat — and you can still dance to it!

THE SONG: Originally a hit for Les Elgart in 1954, it was adopted by Clark as his theme. Lyrics were added by Barry Manilow as a tribute to the influence of America's favorite dance party.

The immortal Dick Clark

Main Cast

Host: Dick Clark

Vital Statistics

90-minute rock'n'roll dance party. ABC.
First aired: Aug. 5, 1957
Most popular time slot: Weekdays, after school.
Last show: Still rocking.

INSIDE FACTS

ABOUT THE PERFORMERS:
- Stars who made their TV debuts on *Bandstand* include: Bobby Darin, The Jackson 5, the Mamas and the Papas, the Osmond Brothers, Dionne Warwick, Isaac Hayes, and lots more.
- The only major rock acts of the '50s and '60s who *didn't* appear on the show were Elvis, Ricky, the Beatles, and the Stones

MISCELLANEOUS:
- In its first year as a national show, *Bandstand* announced a dance contest that brought 700,000 applications in the mail.
- The Beatles' "She Loves You" only got a 73 in "Rate-A-Record," so Swan Records passed up the chance to buy American rights to their other tunes.

TRIVIA QUIZ

If you were watching *American Bandstand* regularly in its early years, you heard these hit records played. Who was singing them?
1. "Puppy Love"
2. "Venus"
3. "The Loco-motion"
4. "Be My Baby"
5. "Will You Love Me Tomorrow"

ANSWERS

1. Paul Anka (1960)
2. Frankie Avalon (1959)
3. Little Eva (1962)
4. The Ronettes (1963)
5. The Shirelles (1960)

Bandstand Boogie

Words: Barry Manilow and Bruce Sussman, Music: Charles Albertine

65

1.,3. We're goin' hop-pin', (Hop!) we're go-in' hop-pin' to-day, where things are pop-pin' (Pop!) the Phil-a-
2. (We're go-in') swing-in', (Swing!) we're gon-na swing in the crowd, and we'll be cling-in' (Cling!) and floatin'

del- phi-a way; we're gon-na drop in (Drop!) on all the mu-sic they play on the
high on a cloud, the phones are ring-in' (Ring!) my mom and dad are so proud I'm on

Band - stand.___ (Band - stand.)___ We're go-in'
Band - stand.___ (Band - stand.)___ And I'll

jump and, hey, I may ev - en show 'em my hand - stand; ___ be-cause

I'm on, be-cause I'm on the A- mer - i- can Band - stand. ___

66

When we dance real slow I'll show all the guys in the grand - stand, ___

what a swing - er I am; I am on A- mer - i- can

Band - stand. ___

3. We're go - in'

Band - stand. _____

That Was the Week That Was

THE SHOW: *That Was The Week That Was* (a.k.a. *TW3*) was the *Saturday Night Live* of the '60s: it was broadcast "live from New York," dealt with topical humor, and featured a regular ensemble of young comedy talent that included future stars David Frost, Alan Alda, Tom Bosley, and Buck Henry. Often very funny and always controversial, it was the first American show to feature cutting political satire. Each week, in a mock newscast (sound familiar?), they would parody current events. And in a revue-style format of short skits and musical numbers, *TW3* lampooned public figures from LBJ to the Beatles. One of *TW3*'s unforgettable segments: silent puppet plays about peace, freedom, and love, staged by Burr Tillstrom, creator of Kukla, Fran, and Ollie.

David Frost hosted TW3 in England and the U.S.

THE SONG: Sung at the show's open and close by Nancy Ames, a member of the cast who became a popular singer. The lyrics actually changed every week, as writers filled in the melody with references to the previous week's news.

Main Cast

Elliot Reid (1st host)	Henry Morgan
David Frost (2nd host)	Phyllis Newman
Alan Alda	Pat Englund
Tom Bosley	Buck Henry
Nancy Ames	Burr Tillstrom

Vital Statistics

Half-hour satire. NBC.
First aired: Jan. 10, 1964
Most popular time slot: Tuesday 9:30 – 10:00 PM (1964—65)
Last show: May 4, 1965
Never ranked in a year's Top 25 shows

67

INSIDE FACTS

ABOUT TW3's ORIGIN:

● It was based on a 1963 British series of the same name, hosted by 24-year-old David Frost.

● The English *TW3* attracted international publicity when a skit in which the Royal Family's barge sank ("And now the Queen, smiling radiantly, is swimming for her life. Her Majesty is wearing a silk ensemble in canary yellow...") prompted a debate in Parliament about banning the show.

● It was adapted to American concerns and aired as a 1-hour special in November, 1963, hosted by Henry Fonda.

● NBC got the greatest immediate response it had ever had for a show, mostly favorable.

● They decided to make it into a regular series a few months later.

TRIVIA QUIZ

THE SUBJECT IS . . .
THE CAST

Can you name the regular *TW3* cast-member who was also a regular on . . .
1. *The Steve Allen Show* (1961)
2. *I've Got A Secret*
3. *To Tell the Truth*
4. *M*A*S*H*
5. *ABC Stage 67*

ANSWERS

1. Buck Henry
2. Henry Morgan
3. Phyllis Newman
4. If you don't know, ask someone
5. David Frost

That Was The Week That Was

Words: Caryl Brahms and Ned Sherrin, Music: Ron Grainer

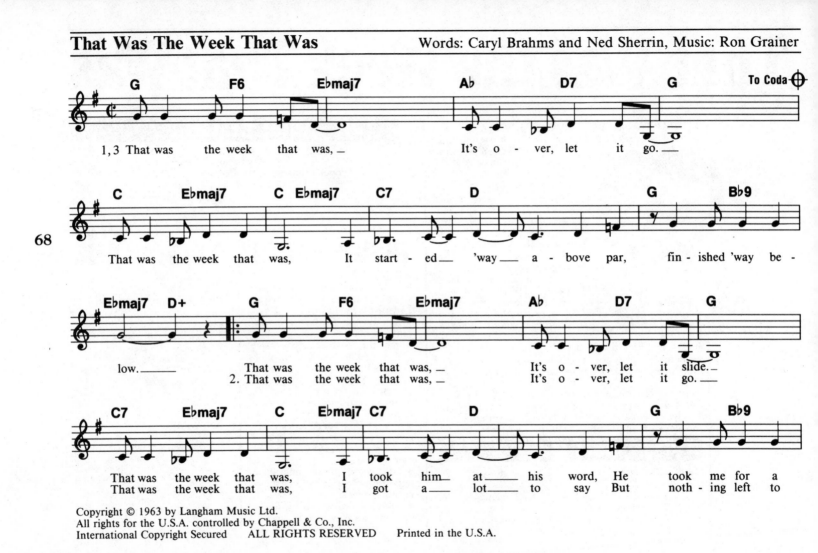

69

The Tonight Show

THE SHOW: *The Tonight Show, Starring Johnny Carson,* is the king of the talk shows. But it's more than that; it's American pop culture in action. Since Carson took over as host in 1962, he has been a major influence in shaping American tastes. When, for example, he appeared wearing a Nehru jacket and turtleneck in the mid-'60s, clothing stores were swamped with people who wanted the outfit, too. When he played a game called "Twister" on the air with Eva Gabor in 1966, it took off overnight, becoming the most successful new game of the decade. When 2 of the Beatles wanted to announce their new Apple Records in 1968, the show they wanted to discuss it on was Carson's (surprisingly, Joe Garagiola was guest host that night. Lennon's first words: "Where's Johnny?"). By the late '70s, Carson had racked up more network hours than any performer in TV history, a record that continues to swell as his show goes on and on.

THE SONG: Co-written by Carson (a talented drummer) and singer/composer Paul Anka. There are no lyrics, but even if you don't read music you can sing it! Ready? And now . . . Here's Johnny!

More than a performer, Johnny Carson is a cultural force in America.

Main Cast

Host: Johnny Carson
Announcer/assistant: Ed McMahon
Band leader: Skitch Hendersen (1962-66)
Milton Delugg (1966-67)
Doc Severinsen (1967-   )
Tommy Newsom (1968-   )

Vital Statistics

90-minute, hour-long talk show. NBC.
First aired (starring Johnny Carson): Oct. 2, 1962
Most popular time slot: Weekdays, 11:30 P.M.–1 A.M.
Last show: Still talking.

INSIDE FACTS

ABOUT JOHNNY'S CAREER:

- After hosting a local L.A. show called *Carson's Cellar* in 1953, and a summer game show in 1954, he got his big break.
- Working as a writer on *The Red Skelton Show* in the 1954-55 season, he was pressed into service as Skelton's one-time replacement when Skelton was injured during rehearsal.
- He did so well as host that he was given a prime-time summer variety show in 1955.
- He then moved to daytime, where he flourished in *The Johnny Carson Daytime Show* in 1956.
- His next program: ABC's game show, *Who Do You Trust?* It became the #1 daytime show.
- When NBC first offered him *The Tonight Show*, to replace Jack Paar, he refused. Then he reconsidered, and took the job.

TRIVIA QUIZ

Can you name some of the more memorable moments in *Tonight Show* history?
1. Ed Ames got one of the longest laughs during a tomahawk-throwing demonstration. What happened?
2. A marriage took place in 1969. Who got married on the show?
3. Carson joked about a shortage of what product, causing a buying panic?
4. Alex Haley, author of *Roots,* surprised Carson with what?
5. What happened when Peter O'Toole flew directly from the set of *Lord Jim* to the *Tonight Show?*

ANSWERS

1. He hit his target dummy exactly in the crotch.
2. Tiny Tim and Miss Vicki Budinger
3. Toilet paper
4. His genealogical chart
5. Exhausted, he became incoherent and had to be led off the stage by Carson

Johnny's Theme (The Tonight Show)

Paul Anka & Johnny Carson

71

AND
NOW...

A Song From A Sponsor

Chock Full o' Nuts Is That Heavenly Coffee

Chock Full O' Nuts is that hea - ven - ly cof - fee, hea - ven - ly

72

cof - fee, hea - ven - ly cof - fee, Chock Full O' Nuts is that hea - ven - ly

cof - fee, bet - ter cof - fee a mil - lion - aire's mon - ey can't buy.

AND
NOW...
A Song From A Sponsor

Brush Your Teeth With Colgate

Written by Robert Forshaw

Brush your teeth with Col - gate, Col - gate Den - tal Cream,___ it cleans your

73

breath (what a tooth - paste), while it guards your teeth._____

The Mickey Mouse Club

THE SHOW: Every day was special on *The Mickey Mouse Club*: Monday was "Fun With Music Day," Tuesday was "Guest Star Day," Wednesday was "Anything Can Happen Day," Thursday was "Circus Day," and Friday was "Talent Roundup Day." Hosted by Jimmie Dodd and "the Big Mooseketeer," Roy Williams, the program was a Walt Disney extravaganza of music, song, dance, cartoons, and adventure serials. The thread that held it together was the mouse-hatted Mouseketeers, many of whom starred in the serials. Among the most popular: "The Adventures of Spin and Marty," "The Hardy Boys," "Annette,", and "Corky and White Shadow." The Mouseketeers were an extended family to kids everywhere. Everybody was on a first-name basis — Annette, Cubby, Doreen, Tommy, and Darlene were like TV friends. At the end of each show, they would sing their sad farewell. Why? Because they *liked* you.

THE SONG: With Mickey leading a parade of Disney cartoon characters, everybody sang along. Except Donald Duck.

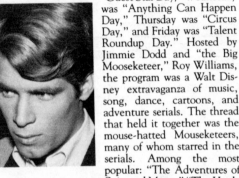

Many young stars began their careers with The Mickey Mouse Club, *including Tim Considine (Spin and Marty) and Don Grady (as a Mouseketeer), both of whom went on to star in* My Three Sons.

Main Cast

Host: Jimmie Dodd
Co-host: Roy Williams
Some Mouseketeers: Annette Funicello, Darlene Gillespie, Carl "Cubby" O'Brien, Karen Pendleton, Tommy Cole, Bobby Burgess, Johnny Crawford, Lonnie Burr, Don Grady, Doreen Tracey, Cheryl Holdridge, Paul Petersen

Vital Statistics

Half-hour and hour-long children's show. ABC/Syndicated.
First aired: October 3, 1955
Most popular time slot: Weekday afternoons.
Last show: September 25, 1959/Still in syndication

INSIDE FACTS
ABOUT THE MOST POPULAR MOUSEKETEER:

• Over 3000 children tried out for Mouseketeer, but only 24 were selected in the first year.

• Of the 24, Annette Funicello was one of the last picked.

• Disney executives thought she was nice, but not especially talented. They expected Cubby O'Brien to be the star of the show.

• Within a few weeks she was getting more fan mail than any Disney star since *Davy Crockett*, surprising even Uncle Walt.

• Even during reruns she received over 1000 letters a week.

• 1959 was her last year as a Mouseketeer. That year she took a role in *The Danny Thomas Show* and had a part in *Zorro*.

• She went on to become a world-famous movie beach-bunny.

TRIVIA QUIZ

1. Which dancing Mouseketeer went on to star in Lawrence Welk's TV show (as a dancer, of course)?
2. What was the chant when it was time to show a cartoon?
3. Where did the Mouseketeers greet their guests on Talent Roundup Day?
4. How could you tell which Mouseketeer was which?
5. Which cartoon character gave lots of advice on the show?

ANSWERS

1. Bobby (Burgess)
2. "Meeska, Mooska, Mouseketeer Mousekartoon Time now is here"
3. At a mock stage depot
4. Their names were on their shirts
5. Jiminy Cricket

Mickey Mouse March

By Jimmie Dodd

Mick - ey Mouse Club! Mick - ey Mouse Club!

1. Who's the lead - er of the club that's made for you and
2. Here we go a - march - ing and a - shout - ing mer - ri -

me? }
ly: }

M - I - C - K - E - Y   M - O - U - S - E!

{ Hey, there! Hi, there! Ho, there! You're as wel - come as can be! }
{ We play fair and we work hard and we're in har - mo - ny! }

M - I - C -

K - E - Y   M - O - U - S - E!   Mick - ey Mouse!   Mick - ey

76

Mouse!   For - ev - er let us hold our ban - ner high!   High!

High!   High!   { Come   a - long   and sing   a song   and join   the jam - bor-
           { Boys   and girls   from far   and near,   you're wel - come as   can

ee!   M - I - C   -   K - E - Y   M - O - U - S - E!_____
be!   M - I - C*   -   K - E - Y**   M - O - U - S - E!_____

* *"See you real soon"*
** *"Why? Because we LIKE you!"*

Top Cat

THE SHOW: The story of a feline Sgt. Bilko and his loyal henchmen (henchcats?). In a lane behind police headquarters in Manhattan's 13th Precinct (right off Mad Avenue), a gang of alley cats have taken up permanent residence. Their leader: Top Cat (T.C. to his friends), a master con-artist and opportunist whose main concerns in life are harrassing assorted humans (like cops, milkmen, and garbage collectors) and coming up with sure-fire schemes to keep his gang safe and comfortable. He's got it down to a science: they always have milk, which they systematically swipe from doorsteps; in bad weather they take refuge in the basement of a nearby deli; and for money, T.C.'s always got a plan. The one thing he can't seem to lick is Officer Dibble, who's made a career out of trying to evict or arrest the gang. The other cats: slow (but not stupid) Benny the Ball, eager Choo-Choo, the brainless Brain, Fancy Fancy the fop, pseudo-intellectual Spook, Pierre, and Goldie. *Top Cat* was a prime-time flop, but kids love it in syndication.

Top Cat's voice was provided by Arnold Stang, perennial TV personality. Remember his ads for Chunky candy?

Main Cast

Character's voices:
Top Cat (T.C.): Arnold Stang
Choo Choo: Marvin Kaplan
Benny the Ball: Maurice Gosfield
Officer Dibble: Allen Jenkins

Vital Statistics

Half-hour animated cartoon show. ABC. Syndicated. 30 episodes.
First aired: Sept. 27, 1961
Most popular time slot: Saturday morning
Last show: Still in syndication

INSIDE FACTS

ABOUT T.C.'S CREATORS, WILLIAM HANNA AND JOSEPH BARBERA

• They created Tom and Jerry for MGM in 1940, in a cartoon called "Puss Gets the Boot." The unnamed cat and mouse were ignored by the studio until the cartoon appeared in movie theaters — where it was a big hit. In fact, it was nominated for an Oscar!

• They began working exclusively on Tom and Jerry, and over the next 15 years, won 7 Oscars.

• One of their most famous pieces: "Anchors Away," in which Gene Kelly's tap-dancing partner is Jerry the Mouse.

• When MGM closed its cartoon studios in 1957, Hanna and Barbera decided to open their own studio and produce low-cost animation for TV.

TRIVIA QUIZ

Test your knowledge of these other Hanna-Barbera shows and characters...
1. Pair of rascally mice
2. Bumbling marshal with sidekick Baba Looey
3. Series based on good-hearted little blue men
4. Penelope Pitstop was a part of these weekly cartoon car races
5. Series based on dot-gobbling video game

ANSWERS

1. Trixie and Dixie
2. Quick Draw McGraw
3. The Smurfs
4. Wacky Races
5. Pac-Man

Top Cat

Words and Music by William Hanna, Joseph Barbera, Hoyt Curtin and Evelyn Timmens

He's the boss, he's a VIP, he's a champ - i - on - ship.__ He's the most tip top Top Cat.

Yes, __ he's the boss, he's the king, but a - bove ev' - ry - thing, __ he's the most tip top Top Cat.

Top Cat!__

79

AND
NOW...
A Song From A Sponsor

Sometimes I Feel Like A Nut

80

81

Winky Dink and You

THE SHOW: *Winky Dink and You* turned viewer participation into an art form — for kids, that is. Here's how it worked: Winky Dink was an animated cartoon boy (with a star for a head) who had adventures with his dog, Woofer. Whenever Winky got into a fix, the show's host, Jack Barry, would call on the audience to save him by drawing a bridge, a rope, or whatever he needed . . . right on the TV screen! In order to do this, kids had to have (and parents had to buy) a Winky Dink Magic Drawing Kit, which included a protective plastic screen that fit over the TV, crayons, and a cloth for erasing. Of course, a lot of kids who didn't own a Magic Screen ended up drawing directly on the TV (including the author — remember, Mom?). Other features: Jack Barry's inept assistant, Mr. Bungle, and a special coded message that was broadcast bit by bit throughout the show (if you didn't have the Kit, you couldn't decode the secret message). This probably wasn't many parents' favorite show, but kids loved it. It lasted for four years, and was revived briefly in the '60s.

THE SONG: A cult favorite today, it was a catchy tune that had kids singing along about their pal Winky in 1953.

Before Jack Barry became a famous game show host, he hosted Winky Dink and You

82

Main Cast

Host: Jack Barry
Assistant: Mike McBean
Orchestra: John Gart

Vital Statistics

Half-hour children's show. CBS. Syndicated.
First aired: Oct. 10, 1953
Most popular time slot: Saturday 11:00-11:30 A.M.
Last show: April 27, 1957. Syndicated 1969.

INSIDE FACTS

ABOUT THE HOST:

● Jack Barry began on TV as host of *Juvenile Jury*, a kids' game show, in 1947. It ran until 1955.

● His second regular TV job was on Joe Dimaggio's 1950 kids' show. Joe interviewed children while Barry assisted. His official title: "Club House Manager."

● Barry moved back to Host for his next outing. The show: *Oh Baby*, in which he interviewed babies. Their answers were dubbed in.

● He became a familiar face on adult game shows in the late '50s, hosting *The Big Surprise, High-Low, The $100,000 Surprise* (co-host with Mike Wallace), *Concentration*, and *Twenty-One*.

● The late '50s scandal in which quiz shows were exposed as frauds almost ruined his career. He couldn't work in TV from 1958-68.

● His comeback: *The Joker's Wild*.

TRIVIA QUIZ

THE SUBJECT IS . . . CARTOON BOYS

Winky was a popular cartoon boy. Can you identify these other classic TV cartoon boys?

1. On *Captain Kangaroo*, he wore a funnel for a hat
2. He was a dog's pet
3. A Japanese robot boy, he had built-in rockets in his feet
4. The red-haired teenage boy who jumped to TV from comic books and had a #1 record
5. A superstrong cave-boy

ANSWERS

1. Tom Terrific
2. Sherman
3. Astro Boy
4. Archie Andrews
5. Bamm-Bamm Rubble

Winky Dink and You

Words and Music: John Gart and John Redmond

Wink - y Dink _____ and you, Wink - y Dink _____ and me, al - ways have a

83

lot of fun to-geth ― er, Wink - y Dink _____ and you, Wink - y Dink _____ and me,

we are pals in fair or storm - y weath ― er. All the kids _____ who heard

Wink - y's mag ― ic word, make a wish and then they all shout "Wink - o" what a big _____

sur - prise   right   be-fore_____ their   eyes,   wish - es   do   come   true   from   say - ing   "Wink -

o",   prest - o,   change - o,   that's   a   thing   of   the   past.   Wink - o,   Wink - o

84

works   twice   as   fast,   Wink - y   Dink_____ and   you,   Wink - y   Dink _____ and   me,

al - ways   have   a   lot   of   fun   to - geth   -   er,   Wink - y   Dink_____ and   you,

Wink - y   Dink_____ and   me,   we   are   pals   in   fair   or   storm - y   weath   -   er.

A Song From A Sponsor

I Love Bosco

Written by Joan Edwards & Lyn Duddy

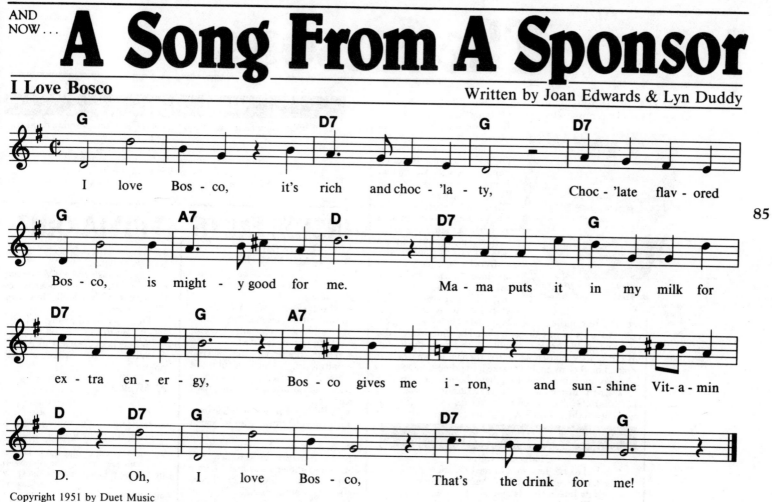

I love Bos - co, it's rich and choc - 'la - ty, Choc - 'late flav - ored Bos - co, is might - y good for me. Ma - ma puts it in my milk for ex - tra en - er - gy, Bos - co gives me i - ron, and sun - shine Vit - a - min D. Oh, I love Bos - co, That's the drink for me!

The Jetsons

THE SHOW: "Meet George Jetson . . ." and welcome to the 21st century, where the only thing that's changed since the prehistoric days of Fred Flintstone is technology; suburbia just keeps rollin' along. The breadwinner of the Jetson family is George, a computer digital index operator at Spacely Space Sprockets ("Yes, Mr. Spacely"); his pretty red-haired wife, Jane, is in charge of their home in the Skypad Apartments; Judy is a typical teenager who's in love with rock singer Jet Screamer and loves to dance the "solar swivel." And then there's Elroy, all-boy. Loves to tinker with his inter-galactic space set. The rest of the household includes their bumbling pet dog, Astro (who was almost replaced by a mechanical dog when he couldn't stop cat burglars), and Rosie the Robot, an out-of-date household helper the family can't bear to scrap. The Jetsons couldn't make it in prime-time, but as a Saturday morning show they have become a perennial. This was the first show ABC ever broadcast in color.
THE SONG: Not much to it, but it's easily one of the best-known themes on TV, judging by requests.

Penny Singleton is best known as the movies' Blondie — but she's been heard on TV since the '60s as Jane Jetson, George's wife.

Main Cast

Characters' voices:
George Jetson: George O'Hanlon
Jane Jetson (his wife): Penny Singleton
Judy Jetson (his daughter): Janet Waldo
Elroy Jetson (his son): Daws Butler
Mr. Spacely (his boss): Mel Blanc

Vital Statistics

Half-hour animated cartoon show. ABC; Rerun on several networks. Syndicated.
First aired: September 23, 1962.
Most popular time slot: Saturday morning
Last show: Still in syndication
Never ranked in the Top 25 shows of a year.

INSIDE FACTS
ABOUT THE JETSONS' SPACE-AGE MACHINES

- One of *The Jetsons'* best features was their space-age gadgets. Here are a few:
- The Food-A-Rack-A-Cycle. A "push-button automat" that automatically delivered any kind of food the Jetsons selected.
- Their home in the Skypad Apartments, which could be "raised or lowered hydraulically to take advantage of the best weather."
- A Seeing-Eye Vacuum Cleaner, with two electronic eyes to search for dirt.
- A Reading Machine. Newspapers and magazines were delivered in micro-tablet form and inserted into the machine, which flipped the pages automatically. By pushing a button, readers could hear photographs talk.

TRIVIA QUIZ

1. What's the Spacely Space Sprocket slogan?
2. Jack Jetwash has a TV exercise program that helps housewives keep a part of their bodies in shape. Which part?
3. From what company did the Jetsons get Rosie?
4. Where does George walk Astro?
5. What's Mr. Spacely's first name?

ANSWERS

1. "Spacely Sprocket, easy on the pocket."
2. Their fingers. From pushing all those buttons, 21st century suburbanites get "Push-button finger" if they're not careful.
3. The U-Rent-A-Robot Maid Service
4. On a treadmill outside their apartment
5. Cosmo G.

The Jetsons

Words and Music by Hoyt Curtin, William Hanna and Joseph Barbera

Meet George Jet-son. Jane, his wife. Daugh-ter Ju-dy. His boy El-roy. And Ro-sy, the Ro-bot Maid.—

87

The Flintstones

THE SHOW: When *The Flintstones* hit prime time in 1960, they started a national craze. TV had finally let cartoons out of the Saturday morning closet, putting them where "respectable" teenagers and adults could enjoy them openly. Everyone watched, and *The Flintstones* became the first cartoon show ever to rank in the top 25 shows of a year. It was essentially an animated version of *The Honeymooners*, with an obvious gimmick — it all took place in the Stone Age. The Flintstones lived in suburban Bedrock (pop. 2500) where Fred commuted to his job at the local quarries every day in his stone-wheeled car (which was foot-propelled). Wilma was the housekeeper, using prehistoric devices like a baby Mastodon vacuum cleaner and shopping for brontosaurus steaks at the supermarket. Next-door neighbors Barney and Betty Rubble shared in most of the adventures. Eventually both couples became parents, and Pebbles Flintstone and Bamm-Bamm Rubble became staples of the Hanna-Barbera Saturday morning cartoon entourage.

THE SONG: Easily the most famous TV cartoon song ever. Everybody likes to sing along with this one!

Alan Reed and Jean VanderPyl, the voices of Fred and Wilma Flintstone

Main Cast

Character's voices:
Fred Flintstone: Alan Reed
Wilma Flintstone: Jean VanderPyl
Barney Rubble: Mel Blanc
Betty Rubble: Bea Benaderet, Gerry Johnson

Vital Statistics

Half-hour animated cartoon show. ABC (1960-66). Syndicated.
First aired: Sept. 30, 1960
Most popular time slot: Friday 8:30-9:00 PM (1960-62)
Thursday 7:30-8:00 PM (1963-64)
Last show: Still in syndication
Ranked in a year's Top 25: 1961 (18); 1962 (21)

INSIDE FACTS

ABOUT ITS ORIGIN:
• When a survey showed that 65% of the audience for Hanna-Barbera cartoons were adults, the company decided to do a cartoon specifically aimed at them.
• Their first idea: a satire on modern suburban life, to be aired in prime time.
• The problem: they just couldn't make it funny enough.
• The magic moment: one of their cartoonists idly drew a picture of a suburban man in a convertible, and gave it a prehistoric look — the fins (this was the late '50s) were made of tree trunks, the roof was thatched.
• As everyone cracked up laughing, it suddenly dawned on them that they'd found the hook they were looking for — Stone Age suburbia!

TRIVIA QUIZ

1. Where did Fred work?
2. What was Fred's favorite meal?
3. Who was Fred's boss?
4. What was the name of the lodge Fred and Barney were members of?
5. Who was the lawyer who never lost a case, who appeared on the show?

ANSWERS

5. Perry Mason
4. The Loyal Order of Water Buffaloes
3. Mr. Slate
2. Brontosaurus burgers and cactus juice
1. The Rock Head and Quarry Cave Construction Co.

(Meet) The Flintstones

Words and Music by Hoyt Curtin, William Hanna and Joseph Barbera

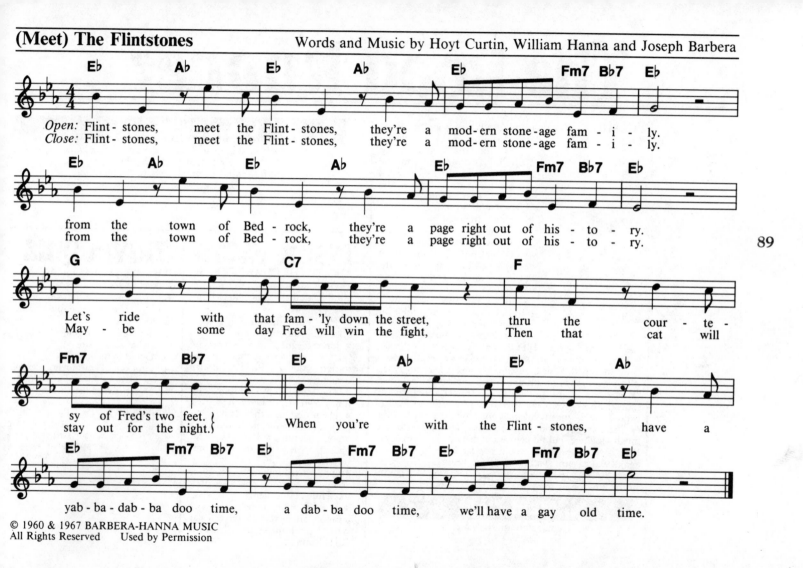

Open: Flint- stones, meet the Flint- stones, they're a mod- ern stone-age fam- i- ly.
Close: Flint- stones, meet the Flint- stones, they're a mod- ern stone-age fam- i- ly.

from the town of Bed- rock, they're a page right out of his- to- ry.
from the town of Bed- rock, they're a page right out of his- to- ry.

Let's ride with that fam- 'ly down the street, thru the cour- te-
May- be some day Fred will win the fight, Then that cat will

sy of Fred's two feet.
stay out for the night. When you're with the Flint- stones, have a

yab- ba- dab- ba doo time, a dab- ba doo time, we'll have a gay old time.

89

The Road Runner

THE SHOW: The theme song calls him "poor little Road Runner," but it's doubtful that Wile E. Coyote would call him that . . . *if* he could talk. Because, as anyone who's ever watched a Road Runner cartoon knows, the Road Runner always wins, and Wile E. always gets flattened, fried, or blasted (usually all three). Every cartoon is the same: the speedy hero (Accelerati Incredibus) is spied as he zooms along the road by his crafty — and hungry — natural enemy (Carnivorous Vulgaris), Wile E. Coyote (let's hear it for the underdog!). Wile E. receives a package from the Acme Corp.

Perhaps the most versatile voice talent in history, Mel Blanc provided the sound effects (Beep-Beep!) in Road Runner

opens it, and surprise! It's an anti-Road Runner device, like a giant rubber-band slingshot rocket-sled missile with a bomb attached. Wile E. assembles it and painstakingly sets it in place, ready to spring the trap and catch his dinner. "Beep-beep!" The smiling Road Runner speeds along, spots the booby-trap, and darts out of danger in the nick of time. Wile E., meanwhile, plummets off a cliff as the bomb explodes in his hands. Some viewers complained of too much violence, but no permanent damage was ever done. Each time, the coyote would pop back up, ready to try again. And again. And again. "Beep-beep!"

THE SONG: Almost a tongue-twister, sung by a chorus as the bird zooms across the desert. "Beep-beep!"

Main Cast

Voice characterizations by Mel Blanc

Vital Statistics

Half-hour animated cartoon show. CBS. ABC.
First aired: Sept. 2, 1967
Most popular time slot: Saturday morning
Last show: Still running.

INSIDE FACTS
ABOUT THE CHARACTERS:

- They were created by Chuck Jones, who is also one of Bugs Bunny's "creators."
- They were introducd in a 1948 cartoon, "Fast and Furry-ous."
- Jones meant it as a parody, but since no one took it that way, he started doing Road Runner straight.
- The coyote was inspired by Jones' own ineptitude with tools.
- He introduced the Acme Corporation because he thought it would be funnier to have mail order gadgets than to see the coyote improvise traps.
- Jones tried giving Wile E. a voice for awhile, but audiences liked him better silent.
- Road Runner is one of the only cartoon characters to have a car named for him — the Plymouth Road Runner.

TRIVIA QUIZ
THE SUBJECT IS . . .
CARTOON BIRDS
Road Runner is a famous cartoon bird. Can you name these other cartoon birds?
1. The talking Magpies
2. Sylvester's desire
3. Donald's nephews
4. Chicken Hawk who doesn't know what a chicken looks like
5. Super-strong duck in diapers

ANSWERS

1. Heckle and Jeckle
2. Tweety Bird
3. Huey, Louie, and Dewey
4. Henery the Chicken Hawk
5. Baby Huey

The Road Runner

By Barbara Cameron

 oad Runner, the coyote's after you.
Road Runner, if he catches you you're
through.

 oad Runner, the coyote's after you.
Road Runner, if he catches you you're
through.

The coyote's really a crazy clown.
When will he learn that he can never
mow him down?
Poor little Road Runner never bothers
anyone.
Running down the road's his idea of
having fun.

Repeat CHORUS

91

Woody Woodpecker

THE SHOW: Woody Woodpecker was already a world-famous bird by the time he pecked his way onto television in 1957 — for seventeen years he'd entertained movie audiences by making trouble for Wally Walrus (and an assortment of other victims), and laughing maniacally whenever he succeeded ("Ha-ha-ha-HA-ha!"). But when he came to TV, several changes were made. First: TV censors insisted on editing out all scenes from his movie cartoons that included "tipsy horses, tobacco-spitting grasshoppers, and neurotic birds." Second: In order to appeal to new viewers, Walter Lantz (Woody's creator) made him cuter and friendlier than he'd been in films. Lantz also appeared on Woody's show as the host, demonstrating animation techniques and introducing other crazy creatures: Andy Panda, Chilly Willy, Gabby Gator, Space Mouse and Charley Bear. But of course Woody always got the last laugh. Ha-ha-ha-HA-ha!!!

Walter and Grace Lantz, the creator and voice of Woody Woodpecker.

THE SONG: A swing-era #1 hit for Kay Kyser's big band in the '40s (pre-TV) and a perennially popular kids' tune.

Main Cast

Host: Walter Lantz

Vital Statistics

Half-hour animated cartoon. ABC, NBC, syndicated.
First aired: Oct. 3, 1957
Most popular time slot: Determined locally
Last show: Still in syndication.

INSIDE FACTS

ABOUT WOODY:
- Walter Lantz's inspiration for creating him came from a real woodpecker that pecked on Lantz's roof until the roof needed replacing.
- When Lantz got frustrated trying to get rid of the bird, his wife suggested it would make a great cartoon character.
- He first appeared in 1940, in an Andy Panda cartoon called "Knock, Knock," and 6 months later was in a cartoon with his name as the title. Instant stardom.
- His voice was supplied by a woman — Gracie Stafford Lantz, the wife of his creator.

ABOUT THE SONG:
- It was introduced in a 1948 cartoon called "Wet Blanket Policy."
- It was the only Oscar nominee ever to originate in a cartoon short.

TRIVIA QUIZ

THE SUBJECT IS . . . CARTOON CREATORS
Woody is a Walter Lantz creation. Can you name the men who created these TV cartoon characters?
1. Fred Flintstone
2. Bullwinkle the Moose
3. Beany and Cecil
4. Mighty Mouse
5. Felix the Cat

ANSWERS
1. Hanna and Barbera
2. Jay Ward
3. Bob Clampett
4. Paul Terry
5. Otto Messmer, or Joe Oriolo (for TV)

The Woody Woodpecker Song

Words and Music by George Tibbles and Ramey Idriss

93

Magilla Gorilla

THE SHOW: Magilla Gorilla, according to a 1964 Hanna-Barbera press release, was born in the small banana-mining town of Simian Springs, Africa. His parents were both professionals — his mother worked in the circus, and his father worked with Albert Schweitzer on several experiments — so it made sense for him to move to Hollywood to become an actor. He was discovered in Schwab's Drug Store, eating a banana split (that's what it says, anyway). In the show, Magilla is a crazy ape who's become a permanent resident of Mr. Peebles' Los Angeles pet shop (where he's on display in the store window). Peebles keeps trying to sell his gorilla, but buyers keep bringing Magilla back. Which makes Magilla — who's got a comfortable rocking chair and his own TV at the store — very happy, but keeps Mr. Peebles in a state of shock. Other characters on the show: Ricochet Rabbit (The Fastest Sheriff in the West), and two Pennsyltucky hillbillies, Punkin Puss and Mush Mouse.

TV veteran Howard Morris, whose credits include Ernest T. Bass on Andy Griffith and The Sid Caesar Show, was the voice of Mr. Peebles.

Main Cast

Characters' voices:
Magilla Gorilla: Allan Melvin
Mr. Peebles: Howard Morris
Ogee: Jean VanderPyl
Ricochet Rabbit: Don Messick
Droop-A-Long: Mel Blanc
Mush Mouse: Howard Morris
Punkin Puss: Allan Melvin

Vital Statistics

Half-hour animated cartoon show. Syndicated 1964. ABC (1966-67).
58 episodes.
First aired: 1964
Most popular time slot: Determined locally.
Last show: Still in syndication

95

INSIDE FACTS

MORE CELEBRITY VOICES BEHIND HANNA-BARBERA CARTOONS:

• In *The Pebbles and Bamm-Bamm Show*, which first aired in 1971, Pebbles' voice was supplied by Sally (*All In The Family*) Struthers, and Bamm-Bamm's by Jay (*Dennis the Menace*) North.

• Harvey (*The Carol Burnett Show*) Korman was the voice of The Great Gazoo, Fred Flintstone's space-man friend.

• When *I Dream of Jeannie* was adapted to a cartoon in 1973, her "master" became Corey Anders, a high school surfer. Corey's voice: Mark (Luke Skywalker) Hamill.

• In the 1972 series, *Jonny Quest*, Jonny's voice was provided by Tim Matheson, star of *Animal House*.

• Other H-B regulars included Dom Deluise, Ross Martin, Gary Owens, Henry Winkler.

TRIVIA QUIZ

Magilla is just one of several TV stars who might've come from Simian Springs. These others each starred in a TV show. Name the show.
1. Judy the Chimp
2. Enoch, Charlie, and Candy (3 show-biz chimps)
3. J. Fred Muggs
4. Chim (a chimp)
5. The Evolution Revolution (a chimp rock group)

ANSWERS

1. *Daktari* (1966-69)
2. *The Hathaways* (1961-62)
3. *The Today Show*
4. *Sheena, Queen of the Jungle* (1955-56)
5. *Lancelot Link, Secret Chimp* (1970-71)

Magilla Gorilla

Words and Music by Hoyt Curtin, William Hanna and Joseph Barbera

96

Eb   Abmaj7   Adim   Eb   Cm7

deal. Don't-cha wan-na l'il go-ril-la you can call your own,— A go-

F7   Bb7   Eb   Ebmaj7

ril-la who'll be with you when you're all a-lone.— Go-ril-la, Ma-gil-la Go-ril-   97

Eb6   *Spoken*

- la for sale. How much is that go-ril-la in the win-dow? Take

Fm7   C7(b9)   Fm7   Ebdim   Eb   Ab

our ad-vice, at an-y price a go-ril-la like Ma-gil-la is

G7(9)   Cm7   Fm7   Bb7   Eb

might-y nice. Go-ril-la, Ma-gil-la Go-ril-la for sale.———

Scooby Doo, Where Are You?

THE SHOW: As a hero, Scooby-Doo isn't exactly Lassie or Rin Tin Tin — he's closer to the cowardly lion in *The Wizard of Oz.* At the first hint of trouble, the large, lovable Great Dane runs in the opposite direction as fast as he can, leving his masters calling "Scooby-Doo, where are you???" Usually Scooby can be found with his head buried under his paws. Scooby and his four high-school pals — Freddy, Daphne, Velma, and Shaggy — spend most of their time cruising around in a vehicle called the "Mystery Machine," investigating and trying to solve mysterious supernatural puzzles. Somehow it's always Scooby — the cowardly canine — who accidentally stumbles on the key clue and uncovers the answer. Whatever Scooby's magic is, it works on real kids, too. He's the star of the longest-running TV cartoon series in history. His show has surfaced as *The New Scooby-Doo Movies, The Scooby-Doo/Dynomutt Hour, Scooby's All-Star Laff-A-Lympics,* and several other incarnations. And there'll undoubtedly be more from Hanna-Barbera.

Casey Kasem is a well-known announcer whose rock shows are seen coast-to-coast. He's also the voice of Shaggy.

Main Cast

Characters' voices:
Scooby Doo (a dog): Don Messick
Freddy (his friend): Frank Welker
Daphne (his friend): Heather North
Shaggy (his friend): Casey Kasem
Velma (his friend): Nichole Jaffe

Vital Statistics

Half-hour, one-hour, 90 minute & two-hour cartoon show. CBS. ABC.
First aired: September 13, 1969
Most popular time slot: Saturday morning
Last show: Currently in production

INSIDE FACTS
ABOUT HANNA-BARBERA STUDIOS:

• It is the largest animation studio in the world.
• In 1957, they introduced their first made-for-TV cartoon series, *Ruff and Ready.*
• Since then they have produced over 250 series, specials, and features.
• Most of their shows are still in syndication. They have been seen by an estimated 500 MILLION people in 80 countries!
• To see everything that the Hanna-Barbera Studios have ever produced, a person would have to watch TV 24 hours a day, every day, for 2 months!
• They have won 8 Emmy Awards, and William Hanna and Joseph Barbera have their own star on Hollywood's Walk of Fame.

TRIVIA QUIZ

THE SUBJECT IS ... CARTOON DOGS

Scooby was one of a long line of TV cartoon dogs. Can you name these other 5?
1. A Shoeshine Boy who became a super-hero
2. Penrod Pooch battles crime disguised as . . .
3. Mr. Magoo's dog
4. Half of the *Oddball Couple*
5. Inventor of the Wayback Machine

ANSWERS

1. Underdog
2. Hong Kong Phooey
3. McBarker
4. Fleabag
5. Mr. Peabody (from *The Bullwinkle Show*)

Scooby Doo

Words and Music by Hoyt Curtin, William Hanna and Joseph Barbera

Scoo - by Doo - by Doo, look - in' for you. Scoo - by Doo - by Doo, where are—

— ya? (O - ver here!) Ev' - ry - bod - y's here wait - in' for you,
Na na na na na na— na na na

could - n't have a show with - out— ya.
na na na na na na na— na. Scoo - by,—

Scoo - bit - y Doo.— Scoo - by,— Scoo - bit - y Doo.—

Hey Scoo - by,— where are you?— (O - ver here!)

Yogi Bear

THE SHOW: If you're visiting Jellystone National Park, be sure to hold on to your pic-a-nic baskets! Because Jellystone is Yogi Bear's home territory — and Yogi ("I'm smarter than the av-er-age bear!") is always devising new schemes to separate campers from their lunches. His cautious accomplice and cavemate is little Boo-Boo Bear ("Hey Boo-BOO!"), who thinks Yogi is the greatest. And his nemesis — usually the only thing between Yogi and a full stomach — is Jellystone's Park Ranger, John Smith. Ranger Smith is determined to catch Yogi, making life more bear-able for park visitors, but most of the time Yogi manages to stay one step ahead of him, proving that Yogi is smarter than the av-er-age ranger, too. Also featured on the show: Snagglepuss, the cowardly lion, and Yakky Doodle, a goofy little duck. On the strength of Daws Butler's voice, Yogi has practically become an American institution.

Daws Butler, the incredible voice of Yogi, Huckleberry Hound, Snagglepuss, Mr. Jinks, Elroy Jetson, Cap'n Crunch, Quick-Draw McGraw, and dozens more

Main Cast

Characters' voices:
Yogi Bear: Daws Butler
Boo Boo Bear (his accomplice): Don Messick
Ranger Smith: Don Messick
Snagglepuss: Daws Butler
Yakky Doodle: Jimmy Weldon
Chopper: Vance Colvig

Vital Statistics

Half-hour cartoon show. Syndicated 1958. 123 episodes.
First aired: 1958
Most popular time slot: Determined locally.
Last show: Still in syndication

INSIDE FACTS

MISCELLANEOUS:
• Yogi's name was inspired by American pop culture hero Yogi Berra, an all-star catcher for the New York Yankees.
• He first appeared on the *Huckleberry Hound Show*, and became so popular that he was quickly given his own program.
• A measure of success: in 1960, a group called The Ivy Three released a novelty record called "Yogi" which reached #8 on the national charts. Sample lyrics: "I'm a Yo-gi. A Yogi bay-bee. Hey Boo-booooo."
• By 1964 he was popular enough for Hanna-Barbera to release a feature-length movie. The title: *Hey There, It's Yogi Bear*.
• He was revived in the '70s in *Yogi's Gang* and *Yogi's Space Race*, fighting pollution instead of snatching picnic baskets.

TRIVIA QUIZ

THE SUBJECT IS . . .
BEARS
Yogi's one of TV's most famous bears. Name these other TV bears:
1. "Only YOU can prevent forest fires "
2. Featured on "The Life and Times of Grizzly Adams "
3. Co-starred with Dennis Weaver in a series named for him
4. Kermit's Muppet friend
5. A bunch of animated bears named Hair, Square, and Bubi

ANSWERS:
1. Smokey
2. Ben
3. Gentle Ben
4. Fozzy
5. The Hair Bear Bunch

Yogi Bear Song

Words and Music by William Hanna, Joseph Barbera and Hoyt Curtin

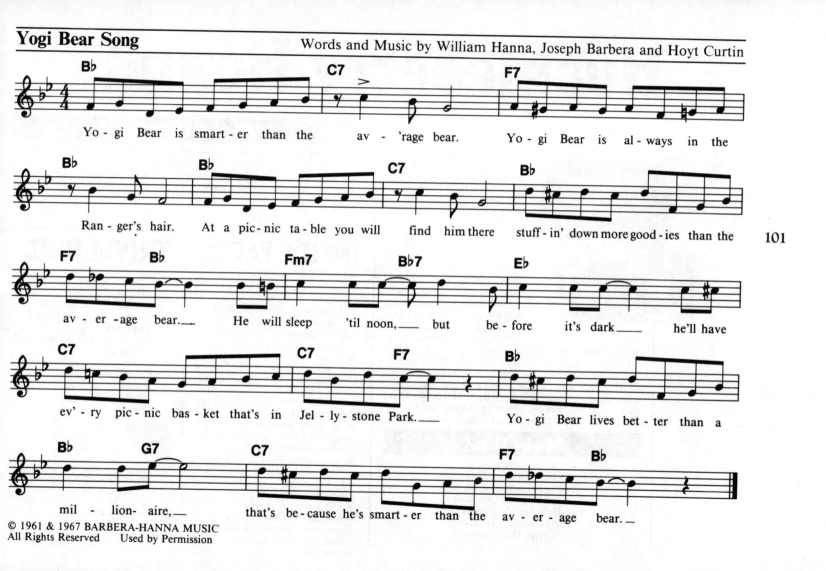

Yo - gi Bear is smart - er than the av - 'rage bear. Yo - gi Bear is al - ways in the

Ran - ger's hair. At a pic - nic ta - ble you will find him there stuff - in' down more good - ies than the

101

av - er - age bear.__ He will sleep 'til noon,__ but be - fore it's dark__ he'll have

ev' - ry pic - nic bas - ket that's in Jel - ly - stone Park.__ Yo - gi Bear lives bet - ter than a

mil - lion - aire,__ that's be - cause he's smart - er than the av - er - age bear. __

Huckleberry Hound

THE SHOW: Huckleberry Hound was TV's first original cartoon superstar. His syndicated show aired at 7:00 P.M., early enough for the kids to catch, but late enough for curious adults to watch too. And they did! Huck was a slow-moving, slow-thinking "canine Don Quixote" who turned up as a different character in every cartoon. In one episode he was in the French Foreign Legion. In another, he was the Purple Pumpernickel, a swashbuckling hero fighting a tyrant who wouldn't let his subjects pay their taxes with credit cards. In another adventure, he was a brilliant scientist who saved America from "an Idaho potato with an evil brain." Whatever the challenge, Huck always proved unstoppable, even if bricks fell on his head ("That smarts ") or he was clobbered by a falling tree ("Man, that was a right heavy tree ") Other characters featured: Yogi Bear, Hokey Wolf, and "those miserable meeces," Pixie and Dixie, taunting Mr. Jinks to distraction ("I hate you meeces to pieces!").

On Huckleberry Hound, Don Messick provided Pixie and Dixie's voices. Other voices: Boo-Boo Bear, Scooby-Doo, Ricochet Rabbit, and dozens more.

Main Cast

Characters' voices:
Huckleberry Hound: Daws Butler
Pixie (a mouse): Don Messick
Dixie (a mouse): Don Messick
Mr. Jinks (a cat): Daws Butler
Hokey Wolf: Daws Butler
Ding: Doug Young

Vital Statistics

Half-hour animated cartoon show. Syndicated 1958. 195 episodes.
First aired: 1958
Most popular time slot: Determined locally
Last show: Still in syndication

INSIDE FACTS

MISCELLANEOUS:

• Huckleberry Hound won an Emmy in 1959 for "Outstanding Achievement in the Field of Children's Programming" — the first animated cartoon to do so.

• It was also popular with adults, however. For example: scientists at the White Sands, N.M. Proving Grounds sent a letter to Hanna-Barbera asking that it be shown later in the evening, so they could see it, too.

• Another example: when the crew of a Coast Guard icebreaker stationed in Antarctica discovered an uncharted island in 1959, they voted to name it after their favorite TV character- — Huckleberry Hound!

• Huck was created to fit a voice invented by Daws Butler — "a Tennessee homespun guy who never got mad, no matter what happened."

TRIVIA QUIZ

**THE SUBJECT IS . . .
EMMY AWARDS**

Huckleberry Hound won an Emmy in 1960 for excellence in children's programming. True or False: each of the following kids' shows has also won an Emmy.

1. *Lassie*
2. *Howdy Doody*
3. *Sesame Street*
4. *Ding Dong School*
5. *Kukla, Fran, and Ollie*

ANSWERS

1. True, in 1954 and in 1955
2. False. Surprisingly, it never did
3. Of course — many, beginning in 1969-70
4. Nope. Poor Miss Francis!
5. True, in 1953 and in 1970-71

Huckleberry Hound Song

Words and Music by Hoyt Curtin, William Hanna and Joseph Barbera

The big-gest show in town, is Huck-le-ber-ry Hound, for all you Guys and

Gals. The big-gest clown in town, is Huck-le-ber-ry Hound, with all his car-toon

pals. It's Huck-le-ber-ry fun, it's for ev'-ry-one,— So come on,— gath-er

'round; Get your-self all set, tune up your T. V. set, for Huck - le-ber - ry

Hound, That oh, so mer - ry, Chuck-le-ber-ry, Huck-le-ber-ry Hound.—

103

Looney Tunes

THE SHOW: "Eh-h-h...What's up, Doc?" And here they are, direct from Hollywood, that zoo-full of zanies you've laughed at since you were old enough to turn on a TV! The "wascally wabbit" — Bugs Bunny, P-P-P-Porky P-P-P-Pig, "wabbit hunter" Elmer Fudd, Yosemite Sam ("Look out varmint, I'm a-warnin' yuh"), Sylvester and Tweety ("I tawt I taw a puddy-tat"), Speedy Gonzales ("Arri-ba, arriba! Anda-lay, anda-lay!"), Daffy Duck ("Thuf-ferin' thuccotash, that'th de-thpicable!"), Foghorn Leg-horn ("Now lissen heah, I say lissen heah boy!"), Henery the Chicken Hawk ("Are *you* a chicken?"), Pepe LePew ("Ooh, my leetle flower"), the Tasmanian Devil, Road Runner, Wile E. Coyote, and ..."Th-th-th-th-th-that's all, folks!"

Cartoonist Bob Clampett, creator of Beanie and Cecil, fashioned Tweety Bird after a baby picture his father took of him.

THE SONG: Surprise! It's a pop tune from the '30s called "The Merry-Go-Round Broke Down," speeded up to sound as crazy as the characters!

Main Cast

All voice characterizations done by the amazing Mel Blanc.

Vital Statistics

Over 350 cartoon shorts. Syndicated, usually with Bugs Bunny or Road Runner as the headliner.
First aired in prime-time: Sept. 28, 1960
Most popular time slot: Saturday morning
Last show: It'll never happen.

INSIDE FACTS

MISCELLANEOUS:
- The name "Looney Tunes" was a take-off on Walt Disney's popular cartoon series, "Silly Symphonies."
- The first Looney Tune, "Sinking In The Bathtub," appeared in 1930. It featured a character called Bosko.
- In the 1935 cartoon, "I Haven't Got A Hat," a little-noticed pig named Porky appeared for the first time, stuttering his way through "The Midnight Ride of Paul Revere."
- In 1937, Daffy appeared in "Porky's Duck Hunt." In his second cartoon, Daffy sang "The Merry-Go-Round Broke Down."
- Bugs first said "What's Up Doc?" to Elmer Fudd in a 1940 cartoon, "A Wild Hare."
- Bob Clampett's '40s inspiration for the Tweety Bird was a baby picture of himself.

TRIVIA QUIZ

1. Which Looney Tune character bounces around, going "Hoo-hoo!"?
2. Pat Boone's last Top 10 hit, in 1962, was named after a Looney Tune character. Which one?
3. Which Looney Tune character was the first to star in an Oscar-winning cartoon, in 1947?
4. Which Looney character is known for saying "Of course you know this means war!"?
5. Which character's name was in-spired by a Campbell's Soup Co. product?

ANSWERS
1. Daffy Duck
2. Speedy Gonzales
3. Tweety Bird ("Tweety Pie")
4. Bugs Bunny
5. Porky Pig (Campbell's Pork and Beans)

The Merry-Go-Round Broke Down

Words and Music: Cliff Friend and Dave Franklin

Intro: Ask me why I'm happy singing like a lark,
And I'll tell you of an old amusement park,
A "Merry-go-round" was there, I gladly paid the fare,
My baby rode around with me then suddenly . . .

Oh, the mer-ry-go-round broke down as we went 'round and 'round, Each
time 'twould miss we'd steal a kiss while the mer-ry-go-round went um-pah-pah, um-pah-pah,
um-pah, um-pah, um-pah-pah, The mer-ry-go-round broke down and made the darn-dest
sound The lights went low, we both said "Oh" and the mer-ry-go-round went

105

106

Mister Rogers' Neighborhood

THE SHOW: As host of the longest-running children's program on PBS, the sweater-clad Fred McFeely Rogers has been a friend and neighbor to American youngsters for over 30 years. Speaking straight into the camera, Mister Rogers establishes a bond of trust rarely found on children's shows. Music is an important part of the rapport; songs like "What Do You Do With the Mad That You Feel" and "When A Baby Comes" help children deal with anger or jealousy. But mostly, Mister Rogers' Neighborhood is fun. Sometimes visitors like Rita Moreno or Marcel Marceau will drop by to say hello.

Mr. Rogers, host of one of America's best-loved children's programs.

And every day, there are visits to the Neighborhood of Make-Believe, whose residents include X the Owl, Cornflake S. Pecially, Daniel Striped Tiger, and Henrietta Pussycat.

THE SONG: One of today's best-known children's themes, it's written by Mister Rogers. Frequently requested by readers for inclusion in this book.

Main Cast

Host: Fred Rogers
Lady Aberlin: Betty Aberlin
Handyman Negri: Joe Negri
Mr. McFeely: David Newell
Bob Dog: Bob Trow
Officer Clemmons: Francois Clemmons
Chef Brockett: Don Brockett

Vital Statistics

Half-hour children's show. NET (1967-70), PBS (1970-present)
First aired: May 22, 1967
Most popular time slot: Determined locally
Last show: Still in production/syndication

INSIDE FACTS

ABOUT MISTER ROGERS:
- He's a Presbyterian minister.
- In 1963, he made his TV debut on *Misterogers* from Toronto, Canada.
- When the show went national in 1968, the name was changed out of concern for children's reading skills.
- He was a pioneer in educational TV — in 1955 he created the first children's program on the first community-sponsored educational TV station in America (Pittsburgh's WQED).
- He's a composer and pianist, writing most of the songs sung on his program.
- He holds 14 honorary degrees from universities and colleges.
- He and Arnold Palmer were high school pals.

TRIVIA QUIZ

Fred Rogers is known and loved by millions of children. So were the hosts of these children's shows. What were their names?

1. *Ding-Dong School*
2. *Super Circus*
3. *The Magic Land of Allakazam*
4. *Wonderama*
5. *Learn To Draw*

ANSWERS
1. Miss Francis
2. Claude Kirschner
3. Mark Wilson
4. Sandy Becker, Sonny Fox, Herb Sheldon, or Bob McAllister
5. John Gnagy

Won't You Be My Neighbor?

1. It's a beau - ti - ful day in this neigh - bor - hood, A beau - ti - ful day for a neigh - bor. Would you
2. (It's a) neigh - bor - ly day in this beau - ty wood, A neigh - bor - ly day for a beau - ty, Would you

108

be mine?— Could you be mine?— 2. It's a be mine?— I have
be mine?— Could you

al - ways want - ed to have a neigh - bor just like you!— I've

al - ways want-ed to live in a neigh - bor-hood with you.___ So

let's make the most of this beau - ti - ful day, since we're to - geth - er we might as well say,

Would you be mine? Could you be mine? Won't you be my neigh - bor?

Won't you please, Won't you please? Please won't you be my neigh- bor? ___

109

Howdy Doody

THE SHOW: Howdy Doody ("Say kids — what time is it?") is one of the most celebrated children's shows of all-time. Hosted by Buffalo Bob Smith ("Y'know, kids — *you* can see *us* on your TV, but did you know that *we* can see *you* too? That's right! Ho-ho-o-o"), it was a circus-oriented puppet show set in the town of Doodyville. The star of the program was a freckle-faced marionette/boy named Howdy Doody who always wore bluejeans and a ban-dana, and was a Good Kid (sort of a juvenile pillar of the community). His nemesis was Mister Bluster, a scheming egomaniac who was also the

The legendary Buffalo Bob Smith and friend

town's mayor. And sometimes it was Clarabell, a seltzer-squirting clown who honked instead of talking. The rest of the Doodyville crowd was pleasantly strange: Flub-A-Dub, for example, was a lovably goofy creature made up of parts of 7 different animals; Dilly Dally was an inept handy-man; Chief Thunderthud was a confused Indian chief who always said "Kowabunga;" etc. The show lasted for 13 years and 2343 performances!

THE SONG: To the tune of "Ta-Ra-Ra-Boom-De-Ay." More kids have sung along with this theme than any other kids' show!

Main Cast

Buffalo Bob Smith: Bob Smith
Clarabell Hornblow (clown): Bob Keeshan,
Bob Nicholson, Lou Anderson

Vital Statistics

Half-hour and hour-long puppet show. NBC. 2,343 episodes.
First aired: December 27, 1947
Most popular time slot: Weekday afternoons and Saturday mornings.
Last show: September 24, 1960

INSIDE FACTS

ABOUT HOWDY DOODY'S ORIGIN:

• In 1945, Bob Smith was a New York radio host. His kids' show, *The Triple B Ranch*, featured a popular character named Elmer.

• Elmer always greeted the listening audience with a "Howdy doody!"

• It was such a popular phrase that when Smith moved to TV in 1947, he used it as the name of his new leading character.

MISCELLANEOUS:

• Smith's home-town was Buffalo, N.Y. — hence his nickname.

• There were actually two Howdy Doodys. The first one, who looked totally different than the second, only lasted a few weeks, disappearing when his creator left in a contract dispute.

• The original Clarabell was Bob "Captain Kangaroo" Keeshan.

TRIVIA QUIZ

1. What was Clarabell's way of communicating?
2. Who was Howdy's twin brother?
3. Who is the Doodyville wrestler trying to *finally* win a match?
4. What was *Howdy Doody*'s original title?
5. What was Mr. Bluster's first name?
6. Mr. Bluster had a twin brother who lived in South America. What was his name?

ANSWERS

1. He honked a horn
2. Double Doody
3. Ugly Sam
4. *The Puppet Playhouse*
5. Phineas
6. Don Jose Bluster

It's Howdy Doody Time

By Edward Kean, Robert Smith and Henry Sayers

Buffalo Bob: Ho-ho-o-o! Well How-dy Doo-dy, boys and girls!
Howdy Doody: Howdy, Buffalo Bob!
Buffalo Bob: Well Howdy, Mr. Doody. And boys and girls at home
in ALL our Peanut Galleries, LET'S GO-O-O!

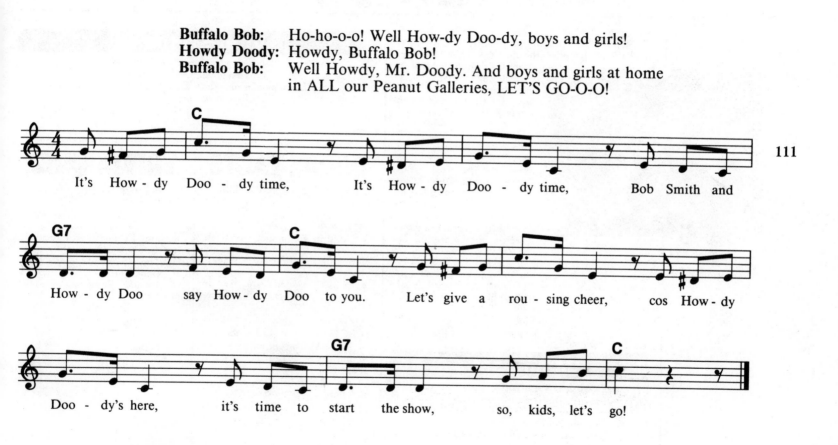

It's How - dy Doo - dy time, It's How - dy Doo - dy time, Bob Smith and

How - dy Doo say How - dy Doo to you. Let's give a rou - sing cheer, cos How - dy

Doo - dy's here, it's time to start the show, so, kids, let's go!

111

Zorro

THE SHOW: Zorro was the Batman of the 1820s, a caped crusader who patrolled the countryside on a stallion named Tornado, fighting injustice and carving a "Z" wherever he went (to strike fear into the hearts of his enemies). The story: Don Diego de la Vega was a wealthy aristocrat studying in Spain. When he returned to his home in Monterey, California, he discovered that the cruel Comandante Monastario had overthrown the legitimate government there. Outraged, Don Diego (who had secretly become a master swordsman) disguised himself as Zorro to do battle with El Capitán and his fat, bumbling sidekick, Sgt. Garcia. Only Bernardo, his loyal "deaf-mute" servant, knew Don Diego's secret identity. Everyone else — especially his embarrassed father, Don Alejandro — thought he was a lazy "playboy." But we knew better, didn't we?

Guy Williams, before he grew a mustache and became El Zorro

THE SONG: It was first recorded by none other than Henry Calvin — Sgt. Garcia! But it was a #19 hit for the Chordettes in 1959.

Main Cast

Don Diego de la Vega (Zorro): Guy Williams
Bernardo (his servant): Gene Sheldon
Don Alejandro (his father): George Lewis
Captain Monastario (his enemy): Britt Lomond
Sgt. Garcia (the captain's ass't.): Henry Calvin

Vital Statistics

Half-hour adventure. ABC. 78 episodes.
First aired: Oct. 10, 1957
Most popular time slot: Thursday, 8:00 – 8:30 PM
Last show: Sept. 24, 1959
Never ranked in the Top 25 of a year.

INSIDE FACTS

ABOUT THE CHARACTER:
• Zorro first appeared in a short story by Johnston McCulley in 1919.
• His first appearance on-screen was in the 1920 movie, *The Mark of Zorro,* starring Douglas Fairbanks, Sr.
• In 1940, the film was remade with Tyrone Power in the starring role.
• Zorro means "fox" in Spanish.

ABOUT GUY WILLIAMS:
• He made an unsuccessful attempt to break into Hollywood in 1952.
• He returned to New York and became a male model instead.
• In the mid-50s he went back to California to try again.
• He won the role of Zorro because he was the only actor trying out for the part who could actually fence.

TRIVIA QUIZ

THE SUBJECT IS . . . HEROES ON HORSES
Zorro's horse, Tornado, was an important part of his image. Here are 5 more TV heroes who depended on their horses. Name the horses.
1. The Lone Ranger.
2. Gene Autry
3. Jim and Joey Newton
4. Little Joe Cartwright
5. Hoss Cartwright

ANSWERS:

1. Silver
2. Champion
3. Fury
4. Cochise
5. Chub

Theme From Zorro

Words: Norman Foster, Music: George Bruns

113

Baretta

THE SHOW: Tony Baretta is one tough cop. I mean, this guy doesn't kid around — he's at war with everyone, from crooks to his stuffed-shirt superiors. And I'll tell ya sum'thin' else — he knows the streets like the back of his hand, so don't try to pull a fast one on *his* beat! Baretta's an undercover cop who lives by himself (except for Fred, the Cockatoo) in a sleazy hotel called the King Edward, right in the middle of L.A.'s crime-infested 53rd Precinct. He grew up on this turf, so he knows how to fit in without being noticed. That makes it easier for him to swoop down unexpectedly and nail the law-breaking crumbs who are overrunning the city. No, he doesn't play by the rules. But as long as he gets results, Baretta couldn't care less who's upset. And in his words, "that's the name of *that* tune!"

Robert Blake, ex-Our Gang kid star, hit the streets in 1975 as Baretta

THE SONG: A #20 hit for the Rhythm Heritage in 1976 ("Don't do it"), but it was sung on the show by another artist — Sammy Davis, Jr.

Main Cast

Tony Baretta: Robert Blake
Billy Truman (his friend): Tom Ewell
Inspector Schiller: Dana Elcar
Lt. Brubaker: Edward Grover
Rooster (Baretta's informant): Michael D. Roberts
Fats (Baretta's informant): Chino Williams

Vital Statistics

Hour-long crime drama. ABC.
First aired: January 17, 1975
Most popular time slot: Wed. 9 – 10:00 PM (1975-77)
Wed. 10 – 11:00 PM (1977-78)
Last show: June 1, 1978
Ranked in a year's Top 25: 1976 (22); 1977 (9)

INSIDE FACTS

THE ORIGIN OF BARETTA:
• When Tony Musante chose to leave *Toma* after the 1973-74 season, ABC decided to replace him with Robert Blake.
• The proposed new title: *Toma, Starring Robert Blake.*
• But *Toma*'s ratings were low, so ABC opted for an entirely new name and location to give Blake the best shot at success.
• They moved it from New York to L.A., and gave the cop a new name — Baretta. It debuted in mid-season, and Blake won an Emmy.

ABOUT FRED THE COCKATOO:
• His real name was Lala.
• He had a stand-in (a stuffed bird) and a double who did flying stunts (named Weird Harold).
• His cage at Universal Studios was equipped with a burglar alarm.

TRIVIA QUIZ

THE SUBJECT IS ...
ONE-NAME COPS

Baretta was a cop known by one name. Name these other "one-name cop" heroes.

1. Raymond Burr in a wheel chair
2. Peter Falk in a raincoat
3. Mike Connors as a tough detective
4. Dennis Weaver as a displaced cowboy
5. Telly Savalas and his lollipops

ANSWERS

1. *Ironside*
2. *Columbo*
3. *Mannix*
4. *McCloud*
5. *Kojak*

Baretta's Theme (Keep Your Eye On The Sparrow)

Words: Morgan Ames, Music: Dave Grusin

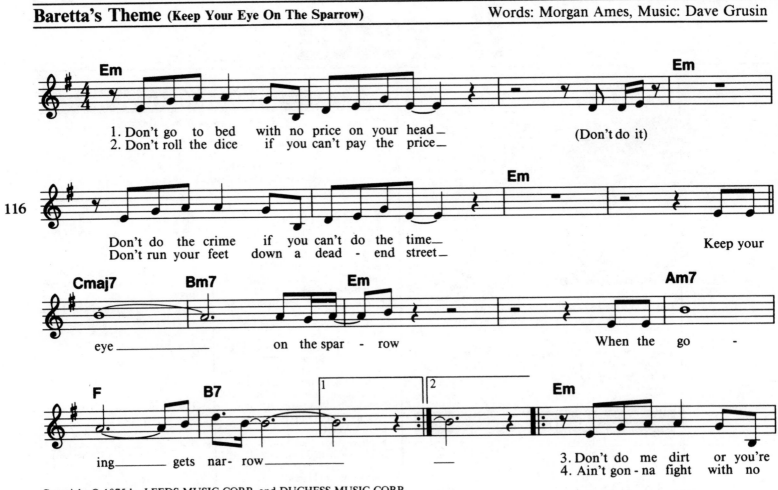

1. Don't go to bed with no price on your head— (Don't do it)
2. Don't roll the dice if you can't pay the price—

Don't do the crime if you can't do the time— Keep your
Don't run your feet down a dead - end street—

eye on the spar - row When the go -

ing gets nar - row

3. Don't do me dirt or you're
4. Ain't gon - na fight with no

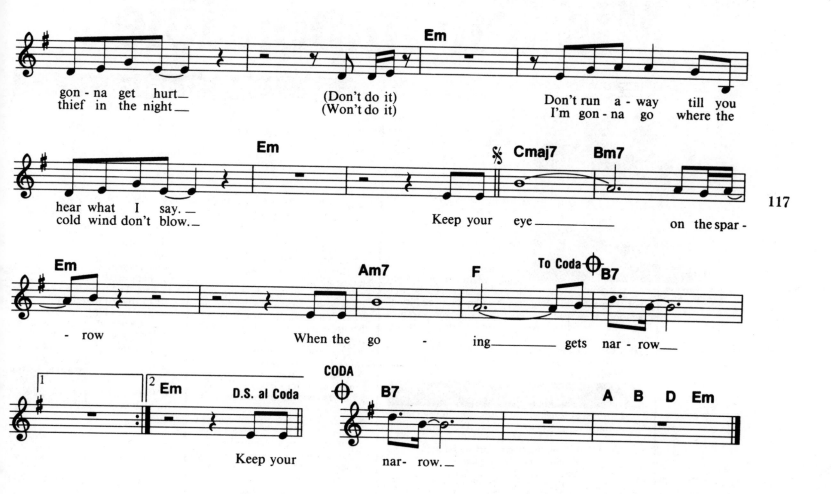

gon - na get hurt___ (Don't do it) Don't run a - way till you
thief in the night ___ (Won't do it) I'm gon - na go where the

hear what I say. __ Keep your eye_____ on the spar -
cold wind don't blow. __

- row When the go - ing_____ gets nar - row__

Keep your nar - row. __

Mission: Impossible

THE SHOW: "Good morning, Mr. Phelps..." At the peak of the '60s spy craze, secret organizations began popping up on TV. There was UNCLE & THRUSH; then CONTROL & KAOS; and finally, the IMF — Impossible Missions Force. Each week IMF leader Jim Phelps could be found in a deserted spot, searching for a bunch of photographs and an exploding tape recorder that would reveal his latest top-secret assignment. "Your mission, should you choose to accept it..." (and he always did) was usually to trick the ruler of some eastern European country or banana republic into sabotaging himself, using an incredibly complex "sting" operation. These wildly unbelievable maneuvers, executed by a team of hand-picked experts, never failed...proving that on TV, nothing is impossible.

Peter Graves starred as Jim Phelps, head of the I.M.F. (Impossible Missions Force).

THE SONG: Composed and performed in 5/4 time by Lalo Schifrin, the instrumental hit #41 on the charts in 1968. With lyrics, it's a complex and beautiful jazz vocal.

Main Cast

Dan Briggs (original I.M.F. leader): Steven Hill
Jim Phelps (replaced Briggs): Peter Graves
THE AGENTS:
Cinnamon Carter: Barbara Bain
Rollin Hand: Martin Landau
Barney Collier: Greg Morris
Willy Armitage: Peter Lupus
Paris: Leonard Nimoy

Vital Statistics

Hour-long adventure/spy drama. CBS. 171 episodes.
First aired: Sept. 17, 1966.
Most popular time slot: Sunday, 10:00-11:00 PM
Last show: Sept. 8, 1973
Ranked in a year's Top 25: 1969 (11)

INSIDE FACTS

MISCELLANEOUS:

- Bruce Geller, the show's creator, cited his favorite movie, 1964 Oscar-winner *Topkapi*, as the inspiration for *M.I.*
- There was little dialogue in the show. Suspense was built by cutting away from scenes to show "ticking bombs, ticking clocks, dripping water, etc."
- This was done as many as 100 times during one show!
- Dialogue was so sparse that in one show, Peter Graves fell asleep while he was in the middle of a scene.
- Graves was selected to replace Steven Hill as I.M.F.'s leader after the first season because Hill, an Orthodox Jew, refused to work after sundown on Friday and Saturday.

TRIVIA QUIZ

**THE SUBJECT IS...
THE I.M.F.**
Each member of the I.M.F. had a separate mission of his own. Can you name it?
1. Peter Lupus made his acting debut in this Annette/Frankie Avalon movie in 1964
2. Landau and Bain starred together in a sci-fi TV show (1975)
3. Leonard Nimoy hosted this documentary show (1976-82)
4. Peter Graves appeared in this movie spoof as a pilot
5. Greg Morris took a gamble as Lt. Nelson in this 1978-81 series

ANSWERS

1. *Muscle Beach Party*
2. *Space: 1999*
3. *In Search of...*
4. *Airplane!*
5. *Vegas*

Mission Impossible

Words: Fred Milano, Angelo D'Aleo, Music: Lalo Schifrin

Fly away, disappear.
I'll be there,
Waiting.

Run high, run low,
Don't stop, go
No matter where
You are bound
I'm around
Waiting,
Hypnotized
On a string,
Following,
Wanting.

Lead me there,
Anywhere.
I don't care.

Cannot stop and I won't stop
Till you're mine.
I keep on dreamin' of you,
No doubt about it
Took my head and made it spin
Somewhere where it's never been.

I'm in a desert,
The middle of nowhere.
With no shoes I calmly bear
Burning coals of fire,
But when I get through
That's when I'll begin to
Undertake a mission that's impossible.

It's said no one can tame you.
Don't give it a try.
You'll fall off if you get up that high.
And deep inside all of your beauty
There is no feeling.
They say you can't be made to laugh or cry.

No, I will have your love.
That's why I'm right. I'll have you.
Run or try to hide, I'll stay beside.
I'm gonna get you.
Get on a plane, go far away, but any day,
I'm gonna get you.

Don't be afraid if you may find
I'm on your mind
Don't try to fight it.
Love's a waiting fuse, you can't refuse
We're gonna light it.

119

The Adventures of Robin Hood

THE SHOW: In 1955, American TV imported a new kind of hero. Instead of cowboy boots, a 10-gallon hat, and a six-gun, he sported pointed slippers, wore a cap with a feather in it, and carried a bow and arrow. He was Robin Hood, the legendary British hero who "stole from the rich and gave to the poor." From their headquarters in Sherwood Forest, Robin and his gang (the Merry Men) waged a guerilla war on the illegitimate ruler of England, Prince John. The result: they became outlaws, relentlessly pursued by the evil Sheriff of Nottingham. Of course the peasants loved them; and so did Maid Marian, Robin's spy in the local government. It all sounds political, but *Robin Hood* was really just a great vehicle for adventure, archery exhibitions, and an outdoor barbeque every night. Hooray for the good guys!

Richard Greene played Sir Robin of Locksley, a.k.a. Robin Hood

THE SONG: As close to a traditional folk song as any TV theme ever came. Recorded by 6 different artists in the '50s.

Main Cast

Robin Hood: Richard Greene
Friar Tuck: Alexander Gauge
Little John: Archie Duncan
Maid Marian Fitzwater: Bernadette O'Farrell
The Sheriff of Nottingham: Alan Wheatley
Sir Richard the Lion-Hearted: Ian Hunter
Prince John: Donald Pleasance

Vital Statistics

Half-hour adventure. CBS. 135 episodes.
First aired: September 26, 1955
Most popular time slot: Monday 7:30 – 8:00 PM (1955-57)
Last show: September 22, 1958
Ranked in a year's Top 25: 1956 (20)

INSIDE FACTS

ABOUT THE SHOW:
• It was inspired by a 1938 movie (also called "The Adventures of Robin Hood") that starred Errol Flynn, king of the swashbucklers, at his peak. Co-stars: Olivia de Haviland, Basil Rathbone.
• Over 500 costumes were used in it, each checked for accuracy by the British Museum.
• It was filmed completely in England. Many of the scenes were actually shot in Sherwood Forest and in Nottingham.

ABOUT ROBIN HOOD:
• His exploits took place in the year 1191, A.D.
• He was featured in two more TV series: Mel Brooks' 1975 sitcom, *When Things Were Rotten*, and a cartoon called *Rocket Robin Hood*, which took place on Sherwood Asteroid.

TRIVIA QUIZ

THE SUBJECT IS . . .
MOVIE HEROES
Many TV heroes appeared in the movies first. Can you name these five:
1. He was played by William Powell in the movies, Peter Lawford on TV
2. Based on a comic strip by Alex Raymond, he was played by Buster Crabbe in film, Steve Holland on TV in 1953
3. In the movies, Elizabeth Taylor loved her. On TV it was Tommy Rettig (and others)
4. Film: Johnny Weismuller, TV: Ron Ely (and others)
5. He and Dale played themselves in movies *and* TV
ANSWERS

5. *Roy Rogers*
4. *Tarzan*
3. *Lassie*
2. *Flash Gordon*
1. *The Thin Man*

Robin Hood

Words and Music by Carl Sigman

Rob - in Hood, Rob - in Hood, ri - ding thru the glen. Rob - in Hood, Rob - in Hood,

with his band of men Feared by the bad, loved by the good, Rob - in Hood,

121

Rob - in Hood, Rob - in Hood.

1. He called the great - est ar - chers to a
2. He came to Sher - wood For - est with a
3. With Fri - ar Tuck and Lit - tle John they

ta - vern on the green, they vowed to help the peo - ple of the king. They
fea - ther in his cap, A fight - er nev - er look - ing for a fight. His
had a rog - uish look, They did the deed the oth - ers would - n't dare. He

han-dled all the trou-bles on the Eng-lish coun-try scene
bow was al-ways read-y and he kept his ar-rows sharp.
cap-tured all the mon-ey that the e-vil sher-iff took,

and still found plen-ty of time to
He used them to fight for what was
And res-cued man-y a la-dy

122

sing.
right.
fair.

Rob-in Hood, Rob-in Hood, ri-ding thru the glen.

Rob-in Hood, Rob-in Hood, with his band of men. Feared by the bad,

loved by the good, Rob-in Hood, Rob-in Hood, Rob-in Hood.

AND NOW...

A Song From A Sponsor

You've Got A Lot To Live

Words by Batten, Barton Durstine & Osborn, Music by Joe Brooks

There's a whole new way of liv - in', Pep - si helps___ sup - ply___ the drive,___

it's got a lot to give___ to those who like to live___ 'cause Pep - si

helps 'em come a - live,_____ It's the Pep - si Gen - er - a -

tion com - in' at ya, go - in' strong, ___ put your - self___

123

be - hind — a Pep - si,   if you're liv - in',   you be - long.—

124

—————————————————— You've got a lot to live,— and

Pep - si's got a lot to give,——————— You've got a

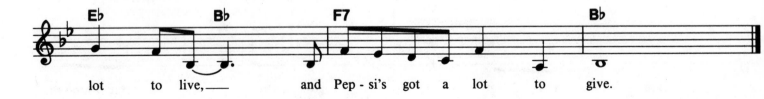

lot to live,— and Pep - si's got a lot to give.

Let's Play Telephone!

A Modern Miracle

Hey, TV fans! Here's great news: now *you* can play TV themes (or at least parts of them) as *well* as sing them... even if you've never played an instrument before! All you need is a push-button phone.

That's right — now the miracle of modern electronics makes it possible for even the worst tone-deaf klutzes to be REAL MUSICIANS. And the best part is, you can do it anywhere, whenever the urge hits you — at home, in the office, even on the street.

Here's How To Do It

1. Pick up the phone (remember: it's got to be a push-button phone)

2. Call a friend (or an enemy, if you prefer). Say "Hey, remember the theme song from (your show here)?" Don't wait for an answer: "Well here it is!" And begin punching the appropriate buttons on your phone. If your friend isn't home, play the song anyway. The ringing provides an interesting background.

When To Do It

A few examples of prime times:

1. Let's say you're mired in a boring phone conversation with someone who just won't take the hint and let you hang up gracefully. No matter what the topic is, just interrupt and say: "Hey! I'll bet you can't guess what TV theme song this is . . ." and begin punching those buttons. That'll do the trick.

2. On the other hand, let's say you're on the phone with someone you're trying to impress (a prospective date, perhaps?) and one of those deadly lulls hits the conversation.

Don't get paranoid. Say "I'm really into music. In fact, here's a TV theme I just learned to play today" and begin punching buttons. It's always a hit.

If You've Got Perfect Pitch:

This may not be for you. The notes aren't exactly right (blame the phone company, not me). But as they say in the music biz, they're close enough for TV themes.

To Get You Started

Here are a few pointers:

1. Sometimes you've got to sing a note or two to fill in for notes that aren't on the phone.
2. Sometimes you can only play a part of a song. That's OK.
3. The numbers are grouped in beats. Two numbers together means you should play them fast.
4. These sample tunes work on Bell phones. I don't know if they work on others.

SAMPLE SONGS
EASY.

Opening four notes of *Mission: Impossible.*　　Opening of *Peter Gunn*
3 – 3 – 9 #　(can be repeated)　　3 – 3 – 63 – 93 – #9 (can be repeated)

INTERMEDIATE.

First 22 notes of *Robin Hood*
(Lyrics: Robin Hood, Robin Hood, Riding thru the glen.
Robin Hood, Robin Hood, with his band of men)
333 – 333 – 999 – 6 – 3
444 – 444 – ### – 8 – 5

Looney Tunes. One note is slightly off.
2 – 0 – 9 – 6 – 2 – 1 (hold)
2 – 0 – 2 – 6 – 2 – 9 (hold)
9 – 9 – 2 – 6
2 – 9 – 2 – 6
2 – 2 – 2 – 6 – 9 – 0 (hold)

ADVANCED.

Popeye. Requires some singing.　　Opening of *Bonanza*
3 – 999 – 6 – 3 9 (hold)　　3 – 333 – 333 – 333 – 3
9 – #6# – (sing) – # 9 (hold)　　# (sing)
9 – # – 6 – # – (sing) – (sing)　　3 – 333 – 333 – 333
– 9 – # – 9 – 3 – (sing)　　333 – 3369# (hold)
3 – 9 – # – 9 – 6 – (sing or 5) – (sing or 7)

Patty Duke Show.　　　　　　　　*Maverick* verse
Begin with chorus: "Still they're cousins . . ."　3 – 396 – 3
000 – 4 (hold)　　(last Chorus only)　6 – 31
0 404　　　　　　　　　　　3 – 693 – – 1 (sing)
0 – 2 – 6 – (sing) – 2　　　　3 – 396 – 3616 (hold)
6 999 – 9 699　　　　　　(sing: "Blowin' up a") 3 –
9 699 – 9 699　　　　　　9 – (sing) (sing) – 6 – 3 (hold)
(sing: "you can lose your") 6
0 – 0 – 4 (hold)
0 404 0 (hold)

Now you're on your own!

TV Theme Song Fan Club

Now, here's the organization you've been waiting for: The Tuneful Viewer's Society for the Preservation of TV Theme Songs — **TV SPOTTS**, for short!

Help preserve the American folk music of the Electronic Era! Join with the tens of thousands of other Americans who are Singing Along, raising their voices together in a chorus of *Mr. Ed* and *Gilligan's Island.* Have an *official* "yabba-dabba-doo time".... Join **TV SPOTTS** Today!

IT'S FREE!
The best things in life ARE free, and **TV SPOTTS** is one of them. All you have to do to become a member — and get your FREE MEMBERSHIP KIT (including the official **TV SPOTTS** CARD!) — is send a self-addressed, stamped envelope to:

> **TV SPOTTS**
> 1201 Olympic Blvd.
> Santa Monica, CA 90404

You've got to include that stamped envelope, because there's no government funding (yet!) for the preservation of TV themes.

Your membership card will entitle you to call up local talk shows and demand that they devote a few hours to discussing your favorite music, to stand on street corners (like I do) with a guitar and serenade passers-by with the theme from *The Patty Duke Show* or *Love Boat,* to sing TV themes in the shower and ignore your neighbors banging on the wall demanding that you stop. And, it's also a great conversation piece or gift. Imagine your loved one's gleeful surprise upon receiving his/her own card in the mail. How thoughtful you are!

Now prestige can be yours...and it's free! Once we're established as a vital force in American pop music, who knows what we can do?

JOIN TODAY! Let your voice be heard, even if it's off-key!

John Javna

Choirmaster

There's More!

If you had fun with this book (and I know you did!), then here are some more books — and a record — you should know about!

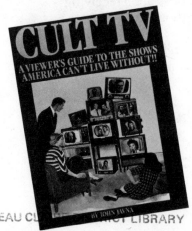